D1291789

Ringside Stories

FROM THE KENNEDY WHITE HOUSE TO REAL ESTATE EVEREST

Richard A. Corbett

WILEY

Published by John Wiley & Sons, Inc., Hoboken, New Jersey.
Published simultaneously in Canada.

For general information on our other products and services or for technical support, please contact our Customer Care Department within the United States at (800) 762-2974, outside the United States at (317) 572-3993, or fax (317) 572-4002.

Wiley publishes in a variety of print and electronic formats and by print-on-demand. Some material included with standard print versions of this book may not be included in e-books or in print-on-demand. If this book refers to media such as a CD or DVD that is not included in the version you purchased, you may download this material at http://booksupport.wiley. com. For more information about Wiley products, visit www.wiley.com.

Library of Congress Cataloging-in-Publication Data:
ISBN: 978-1-118-89872-7 (cloth)
ISBN: 978-1-118-89881-9 (ePDF)
ISBN: 978-1-118-89903-8 (ePub)

V10014747_102219

I wrote this book for my family—my wife Cornelia, our children, and grandchilden—Heather, married to Bill Amenta, living in Brooklyn with grandchildren Lukas and Eloise; Cori (now Lamara) married to Timothy Tillman, living in Santa Barbara; Alyda, married to Stephen Porter, living in Austin; and Rick, married to Jennie, living in Tampa with grandchildren Will, Ben, and Emily. I am so proud of all of them and love those grandkids!

Contents

Acknowledgments

This book is my story—but it was made possible because of the people who helped put the pieces together, aggressively encouraged me, and followed up with the technical realities of producing a publishable manuscript. During the production of this book, Cornelia, my wife, played her usual, critical role, getting me to fact check and cut out the fluff. Local Tampa journalist Paul Guzzo assembled and transcribed recorded interviews to craft the draft document. My friend Jay Wolfson edited and finalized the manuscript and coordinated production with editorial and production staff at Wiley, my publisher. Jay Hughes provided constant encouragement and substantive suggestions. The recollections of Joe Hakim, past Kennedy Office CEO, helped to clarify my memories. Julie Strauss Bettinger offered import guidance on style. My office staff made sure that the background and process components functioned: Jennifer Kent kept all of the people and communications coordinated; Melanie Craig knew where to find all of the critical source documents; and Christy Martineau provided all of the backup and cover.

My mother did not live long enough to share most of my life experiences. My father was a role model and a compelling, often involved force behind many of my successes.

Prologue

On June 6, 1968, when I was half-naked, sitting alone next to Bobby Kennedy's murdered body in the Los Angeles morgue, I could not have imagined that 50 years later I would be fabulously lucky in life and successful beyond any measure. I overcame the gut punch of Bobby's death, along with subsequent challenges through life lessons and skills learned from boxing, scouting, the outdoors, and complex parents. These skills prepared me for the deep immersion in the political and financial dealings of the Kennedy family and the hard-knock world of high-stakes real estate deals.

Friends told me I should capture my story to share with my children, grandchildren, and friends. So I started writing, recording, and remembering. And as I did, I recalled things I had not thought about for decades: boxing matches and punches in the face; Nixon's remoteness versus John F. Kennedy's intimate charisma; business deals gone haywire; and crazy, sometimes foolish, and often scary events that, taken all together, brought me the gifts of a loving and dynamic wife, happy and engaged children and grandchildren, and true friends. The story of my success includes bumps, bruises, and epiphanies from the lessons I have learned.

The metaphor of the boxing ring has been an active, almost daily part of my life. It is how I often viewed and dealt with the equally brutal ring of business and real estate within and outside the Kennedy family's financial world. The outdoors and scouting were both foundational growth experiences and touchstones of sanity, needed while growing up in the home of an alcoholic mother and a driven and successful political father. The horror of Bobby

Kennedy's murder, which I witnessed firsthand, has been my benchmark for a dramatic life transition and a continuing connection to the brilliant and tumultuous financial successes of the Kennedy family. These experiences led to the struggles and success of my real estate business, and to the enjoyment of my family life. I share the bona fide drama—and also the lessons learned.

1

Robert Kennedy Is Buried in My Clothes

I n 1968, I was a young, hotshot political wannabe. It was my good fortune to be close to one of the most prominent families in American politics—the Kennedys. They were my friends and mentors. Beginning in the summer of 1960, following my graduation from college, I worked as a runner on the floor at the Democratic National Convention that gave John F. Kennedy the Democratic presidential nomination; I later became a member of JFK's presidential transition team and staff. I also served as a member of Ted Kennedy's campaign team, and as assistant to the manager of the family's business office in New York City. By the time I was 30, I'd been named national treasurer for Robert Kennedy's 1968 presidential election campaign and envisioned a long political career in the White House once Bobby became president. The world was mine for the taking.

Or so I thought.

On June 4, 1968, I was in Los Angeles, California, with Bobby and the entire campaign team. The primary polls had been closed for four hours. It had been a stressful few days gearing up for California's presidential primary. I was supposed to be in charge of managing the money for a campaign that was financially out of control. We'd blown our budget in every primary prior to California's, and the campaign team was still spending recklessly. I tried numerous times to explain that campaign donors expected us to be more responsible and that spending family money on the campaign was borderline illegal. But the higher-ups—Bobby included—told me to keep quiet. The only thing that mattered, they said, was winning. And the campaign would break the bank if that was what it took. By the time we made it to California, the free spending—not to mention the verbal abuse—was beginning to weigh on me. But the California polls, so critical to national success, looked good. That helped the campaign as well as my ego.

That evening the team was upstairs in one of the rooms at the Ambassador Hotel when an exuberant Bobby Kennedy came bursting through the door with the good news. He had won the California Democratic presidential primary, defeating Eugene McCarthy. Although he was still behind in the national Democratic polls, his victory in California could swing the Democratic nomination, and Bobby knew it. Once he won that nomination, there was little doubt he would defeat whomever the Republicans tossed into the ring. "My God," he told everyone in his classic Boston accent, "I'm going to be the next president of the United States."

He was right. He could not lose. People loved Bobby. They connected with him. I believe there were three things, in particular, that drew people to Bobby Kennedy:

1. He had a glowing, magnetic charisma. And with that positive energy came a remarkable projection of confidence, competence, and inspiration.
2. He fostered a powerful and deep loyalty. Those who worked for him believed in him completely, and he trusted those of us who were within his inner circle.
3. He had a strong sensitivity to underdogs. Maybe this was because he had been something of an underdog growing up, always second to his brother Jack (JFK) and to the shadow of Joe Jr., the eldest son and golden child until his death in World War II. Bobby was handsome, but not as striking as Jack. He was a good athlete, but not as competitive as Jack. He was a good public speaker, but not as captivating as Jack. Bobby always felt (as did many others) that after Joe's death, Jack became the golden child and that Bobby became second best. I believe this drove Bobby to become one of the hardest workers I have ever met. It impelled him to want to become president of the United States.

After Bobby briefly celebrated the primary win with his campaign team, it was time to announce the victory to the world, which he would do in the Ambassador Hotel's ballroom, where Democrats were gathering for the presidential primary celebration. All the national networks were there, along with a number of celebrities. The Kennedy inner circle included entertainer Andy Williams, writer George Plimpton, Olympic decathlon gold medalist Rafer Johnson, and professional football player Rosey Grier.

I was on stage with Bobby as he addressed his supporters. He looked every bit the part of a future president of the United States as he picked up the microphone and said thank you to the cheering crowd. Bobby was good on TV.

He spoke eloquently yet forcefully, as a president should. He spoke about peace in Vietnam, about bettering America, and about making the entire world a safer place. He pounded the pulpit with his index finger, a gesture he often used when he was fully connected, both emotionally and intellectually, his voice rising as his supporters grew more and more enthusiastic.

Adding to his allure that evening was the presence of Ethel, his stunning wife, wearing a pearly white dress with shoulder straps and a few dark stripes, glowing with pride as she stood just behind Bobby's right shoulder.

When he said, "On to Chicago, and let us win there"—a reference to the Illinois primary scheduled to take place one week later—the cheers nearly blew the roof off the place. It was a call to solidarity and victory and it created a rush I can still feel today.

Following the speech, Bobby turned to Steve Smith, his brother-in-law and campaign manager, and Bill Barry, his New York security chief, and told them he wanted to go out the back way because he was too tired to negotiate the crowd. It was already after midnight. Ethel agreed to go out the front door and to meet him at the car. She went on her way and we went on ours.

Though decades have passed, I can still replay the next few moments in slow motion. Bobby, Smith, and I cut back through the kitchen together with some of the celebrities, plus a few others, including members of the press. On one side of us was a row of stainless-steel work tables littered with dirty dishes; on the other was a row of silver ice machines, at the end of which was a portable tray stacker.

Bobby shook the hand of one of the kitchen busboys, a skinny 17-year-old Mexican with angelic eyes who was wearing a white uniform. As their hands touched, a small man with a .22-caliber revolver stepped out from behind the tray stacker. I was standing over Bobby's right shoulder, so I saw the gun clearly, but I did not react. It did not seem real. First of all, the man holding the gun did not look threatening. He wore a pair of worn jeans and a short-sleeved, button-down shirt and had thick and well-cropped hair. There was nothing evil-looking about him.

But what does a killer look like? In real life, the bad guys do not wear black capes and twirl their mustaches.

It happened so quickly and the man looked so unassuming and harmless that for a split second, I thought it was a joke—as if some clown were reenacting a scene from *Gunsmoke* for our amusement. Nothing I saw could make me believe that I was witnessing the assassination of my friend and one of the nation's brightest minds.

Bobby was the only one who seemed to react when he saw the gun. It might have been instinct, given what had happened to his brother Jack five years before. He ducked and turned to the left, but at such close range, half of the bullets caught him anyway. By the time the maniac was done unloading the cylinder, he'd hit Bobby three times, once behind his ear, once in his chest, and once in the back of his neck. Several other people had also been hit.

Bobby crumpled to the floor, and the busboy, clearly in shock, found himself cradling Robert Kennedy's bleeding head in his hands. I remember bending down and loosening Bobby's tie just as the athletes Grier and Johnson were overpowering the gunman, Sirhan Sirhan, and grabbing the spent weapon from his hand.

It was mass chaos, with camera men, kitchen staffers, and Kennedy supporters all running urgently in different directions, made more confusing by the background sound of the loud clattering of objects in the crowded kitchen.

Some of the press members started snapping photos of the downed presidential candidate. One photo showing the busboy holding Bobby in his arms became the most remembered of all the others taken that day. When the teenager moved his hand from behind Bobby's head, the gravity of the situation hit me. Blood was everywhere, and we were assaulted by the smells of gunpowder and burnt human flesh. The Hollywood crowd—Williams, Plimpton, and the rest—were crying, unable to do anything. The shock for all of us was overwhelming. In that endless moment, the brutal truth finally sank in: Robert Kennedy was going to die.

Ethel rushed in, pushing through the sea of reporters. Bobby was still alert and promised her that everything would be okay. But I was close enough to see the wounds he'd sustained, and I could feel the truth. In that surreal scene, as life began to drain out of his wounds, we all stood by, powerless—at once expecting that surely something would save him, yet paralyzed by the possibility that he was not going to make it. I watched him breathe and bleed, then begin to slip away. I remember feeling sickened as the energy, the charisma, the power, the hope—the very life of the man I knew—wavered and waned in front of me.

Somehow, despite the chaos, Steve Smith kept his cool. Just as he had throughout the campaign, he barked out orders in a no-nonsense tone. We were told to take Bobby to the Good Samaritan Hospital across the street. An ambulance arrived outside and Bobby was put on a stretcher. I was instructed to stay with him, and I followed him and the medical attendants to the elevator.

When these types of dramas play out in the movies, you're used to things turning out okay. For us, it was the exact opposite. First, the elevator broke. I don't know if it stalled for five seconds or five minutes—it seemed like an eternity—but during that time Bobby started trembling from the shock and he slipped out of consciousness. Then, after the elevator doors finally opened and we got him to the waiting ambulance, the driver took him to the wrong hospital. The Good Samaritan, which had the staff capable of treating such a trauma, was across the street from the hotel, but for some reason Bobby was taken to the Central Receiving Hospital, which was located a mile away.

More than 30 minutes after arriving at the wrong hospital, Bobby was taken back to Good Samaritan. The doctors there tried to save his life, but it was far too late and the damage too profound. I recall thinking that he'd been doomed the moment the three bullets hit him. There was no surviving that sort of attack.

Robert Kennedy was officially pronounced dead at 1:44 a.m., June 5, 1968. The Los Angeles coroner, Dr. Thomas Noguchi, was required to perform an autopsy on the body and Smith told me to stay with Bobby—the family wanted somebody they knew and trusted with him at all times. I stayed in the basement, where the morgue is located, the rest of the night, as the coroner split my friend's body wide open and removed his organs. Decades later, I can still recall the stomach-churning smells of gastric acid and embalming fluid that marked those early morning hours.

Moments after the embalming fluid had set, and the undertaker and his assistant had arrived with the coffin, Steve Smith phoned to inform us that Ethel and Jackie were on their way downstairs and they wanted the body immediately.

He was not exaggerating. Minutes later a loud banging echoed through the basement. The Kennedy family was outside, pounding on the door. They were ready to take the body.

There's one thing you learn fast working with the Kennedys: When they want something done right away, it had better get done. Moving a family member's dead body was no exception. They wanted the body placed in the coffin and moved immediately.

There were two minor obstacles. First, we didn't have any clean clothes for Bobby; everything but his suit jacket was stained with blood. I was his size, or close enough. I took off my shirt, tie, pants, and belt and we dressed Bobby in my clothes. Teddy Kennedy came in, giving his cuff links, shoes, and socks to the cause, and we thought we were ready to go. Then a second problem arose—the body was already stiff from the rigor mortis. Because of the position of his arm, we couldn't fit him into the coffin.

By then, Jackie and Ethel were on the other side of the door, knocking louder and louder with each second that passed. Smith came rushing in and told us we had to leave. When I told him that the body was frozen into an awkward position and we couldn't get him into the coffin, he said he didn't give a damn and told us to figure something out.

The undertaker was overwhelmed by the circumstances and unable to come up with a solution. I took the lead. I tore the lining out of the coffin and ripped all the stuffing away, creating more room for the body. The undertaker had a look of horror on his face, until he saw that it was going to work. We placed the body in the coffin, forcibly cramming the arm inside. Once he was inside the wooden box, a twinge of guilt came over me. We were tossing Bobby's body around as if it were a mannequin. I looked into Bobby's eyes. The light that drew so many people to him was gone. His body was now just a shell, his soul ripped out of him by a maniac. But there was no time for mourning. I closed his eyes and latched the coffin, wrapped a blanket around myself, then opened the door to let the family in.

They took the coffin, loaded it into a van, and drove it to a waiting plane.

I don't recall how I got back to my hotel. I was nearly naked. I must have been given a ride, because I cannot imagine that I caught a cab or walked through the streets that way.

The following morning, I flew all the way back to New York, along with many of the core staff. On the flight, I was shocked to witness important members of the team contacting the campaign of Minnesota Senator Hubert Humphrey—previously Bobby Kennedy's biggest rival.

Politics makes strange but pragmatic bedfellows.

On June 8, 1968, I was part of the funeral train that traveled from St. Patrick's Cathedral in New York to Arlington National Cemetery in Virginia, stopping in towns along the way to greet mourners. At the end of that exhausting procession, when Robert Kennedy was finally laid to rest, he was still wearing my clothes.

For the next week, the nation wept, and I had to wake up from my dream of Camelot. While the American people mourned the murder of a great American, I struggled with the loss of a friend, the end of an era, and the death of a personal ambition. It was an ambition that the Kennedys had helped create and which had fueled a dream—one that had seemed so compelling, so unstoppable. For almost a decade I had hitched my wagon to the Kennedy family, seeing them as my ticket to a high-profile career in the White House. With the death of Bobby, that was no longer a possibility. I would have to redefine my career and myself. That reality struck me hard and was painful.

Perhaps I sound shallow, cold, and selfish when I focus on my own future in the aftermath of Bobby's death. Let me be clear: Bobby Kennedy was my friend and I was, and still am, devastated by his death. As those on the plane back from Los Angeles had done when they tried to hook up with the Humphrey campaign, I had to quickly reorient my life. I was still alive and had to move on.

After Bobby's funeral, I woke up in New York with new clothes and nightmarish memories. I was struck by an unusual level of clarity that my world was going to be wildly transformed. My earlier plans and expectations were dashed, and I would be launching myself on a new course, motivated—indeed, driven—by his death and by my friends in the Kennedy family. I could no longer be content with riding others' coattails. Although I had earned my position with the Kennedy family, I realized I had been too dependent on their success. Once aware of that fact, I knew I had to create my own future.

But my trajectory from that tragic moment was equally shaped by the dynamic forces of my own family and by a separate history that literally gave me life. Those beginnings had played out in Brockport, New York, a small upstate village on the Erie Canal.

CHAPTER 2

My Father Was a Bona Fide Hero

Donald James Corbett's big American dream wasn't going to come true in Brockport, New York, the town where he was born in 1903. He wanted to attend college. And not just any college—he had set his sights on Notre Dame University. He wanted to take his athletic ability to the grandest stage in the country—the Fighting Irish's football team—while earning a degree.

My father was raised on High Street in a home barely large enough to fit his parents and six children. I went to see the house when I was a kid and it reminded me of a Halloween witch house. It was falling apart and leaning to one side as though the slightest breeze could blow it over. It had peeling paint, cracked windows, splintered siding, and a lawn with nary a green spot in sight. Decrepit as it was, for my father the house was something special—indeed, magical. To him, it was the home that allowed his father, John E. Corbett, to build his own American dream, much the way my father's grandfather, James Corbett, had done.

My great-grandfather's American dream was a simple one: to make it to America alive so his children could grow up in the land of opportunity. He came to the United States from Ireland in the 1870s with his family, which included my five-year-old grandfather, E.J. Corbett. They took passage on a cargo vessel in less-than-comfortable accommodations. There were no bedrooms, only boarding quarters, which were giant rooms lined with hundreds of dusty and rusty bunks. The shipboard meals were equivalent to what's served in prisons today. The boat had no heating or air conditioning and was easily tossed about by the angry seas. The journey took weeks to complete.

Many of the passengers died en route. Some succumbed to the extreme heat or cold; some died of food poisoning or malnutrition caused by unsanitary cooking and food storage; others were felled by illnesses that worsened because of lack of proper medical attention; some were lost overboard during rough weather. Like other immigrants, my great-grandfather was willing to endure these tough conditions in order to get a shot at the American dream.

He was lucky; none of his family died on the long and perilous journey. They disembarked in New York and traveled to Brockport, a small village that thrived as a port on the Erie Canal. In the mid- to late 1800s, immigrants from Europe, primarily Irish, flocked to the village to take advantage of the many employment opportunities offered by the canal.

Brockport's population was only a few thousand. Roads were unpaved, horses were the main source of transportation, and kerosene lanterns illuminated the village's main street, which consisted of a handful of mom-and-pop establishments. Farming communities growing fruits and grains surrounded the village. These crops were shipped throughout the country from Brockport via the railroad and the Erie Canal.

The canal was central to the economy and to the growth of upstate New York, and, for that matter, to much of the northeastern United States. It provided the principal means by which commodities ranging from food to raw materials and finished goods were transported from farmers and producers to factories and customers. For those living and working near it, the canal was the lifeblood of their world.

I've not been able to find out what my great-grandfather, James, did for a living, but when my grandfather, John E. Corbett, was old enough to work, he became a cooper, someone who made barrels that were packed with supplies for the boats docking at the port or used to ship supplies from one canal work station to the next.

My grandfather had a pond in his backyard on which he built a sawmill that he used to make barrels. He also sold ice. When the pond froze, he would cut the ice, place it on a sled pulled by horses, and deliver it door to door throughout the village.

I love the stories of first-generation immigrants like my grandfather. They came to America asking themselves, "What can I do to make a living?" And, more important, "What can I do to make life better for my children?" What grew among these immigrants was a powerful loyalty to the United States, their new home. While they may have been Irish in heritage, they quickly identified as being American.

This was the world into which my father, Donald James Corbett, was born. And part of my grandfather's American dream—a big part—was to see a family member graduate from college. That dream was placed squarely on my father's broad shoulders.

As far back as my father could remember, he was a working man—selling ice and making barrels for my grandfather. That work ethic turned my father into a dynamic physical specimen. He had a wiry build, with blue-collar muscles, not the fitness club muscles many men build today, the kind that enable a man to lift a lot of weight when it's bolted neatly to a bar. Blue-collar muscles empower a man to tear a battery from a car with his bare hands. My father was all blue-collar muscle and he used his physical prowess to become one of the best athletes in Brockport and the surrounding area, starring on his high school's baseball, basketball, track, and football teams, with the latter being his strongest suit. Photographs reveal him as a dashing young man and his grades testified to his intelligence. People who knew him then said he was one of the most popular teens in Brockport, the big man on campus, recognized everywhere he went.

Dad's dream of attending Notre Dame was not that special. It was similar to those of thousands of other young boys, especially Irish-American boys. Young men throughout the United States dreamed of wearing those gold and blue colors and running out onto the football field surrounded by tens of thousands of screaming Fighting Irish fans. But only the most select athletes had the talent to realize that dream. My father *did* have the talent, but Notre Dame did not recruit him. The coaches did not come to him and ask him to play, so he decided to go to Indiana and introduce himself to them. My father's locally demonstrated talent was dwarfed only by his courage and self-confidence.

Having so little money, he could not afford the direct train fare to Indiana, but he packed all his clothes into a dingy duffle bag and hit the road for Notre Dame. He took a train as far as he could afford, and then walked and hitchhiked the rest of the way. Though he traveled through only five states, the trip took weeks. When he finally arrived at Notre Dame, he marched into the admissions office, showed them his high school transcripts, and told the admissions officers that he wanted to apply. He had the grades to be eligible, but he did not have the money for tuition. Many would have given up at that point. Not my father. He was determined to attend Notre Dame, play football, and earn a degree.

He found lodging at Corby Hall, a dwelling used primarily by priests who taught at Notre Dame. It was also used for students when campus housing became too crowded. Though my father was not yet a student, the nuns who ran the hall didn't have the heart to turn him away after hearing that he'd traveled so far for a chance to attend the university. They swept a bird's nest out of a corner of the hall's basement and allowed him to sleep there while he got on his feet financially. It was supposed to be only a short stay. It turned into a three-year residency while he earned money for tuition by working in the campus cafeteria.

Finally, in 1924, at the age of 21, he had his tuition money and fulfilled one third of his dream—he was attending Notre Dame. He quickly got to work on the rest—playing football for the school and earning a degree.

Notre Dame's football program encouraged walk-ons back then, so my father knew he had a chance to make the team. Before the first tryout, he approached head coach Knute Rockne, now regarded one of the greatest college football coaches of all time, and asked him what it would take to earn a spot on the team. Rockne, not one to mince words, looked over the wiry, blue-collar-muscle-bound, five-foot-nine-inch, 170-pound upstart and said, "If you can throw, catch, run, and tackle, you'll play football for Notre Dame. There's nothing else that matters. You can't fake talent. If you have it, you'll play for this team."

My father made the team, earning the backup quarterback spot. He kept that position for four years, playing for two of Notre Dame's most famous teams: the 1924 squad, renowned for its Four Horsemen, the name for the team's talented backfield, consisting of Harry Stuhldreher, Don Miller, Jim Crowley, and Elmer Layden, who led the team to an undefeated season; and the 1928 squad, best known in Notre Dame lore as the year Rockne delivered his "Win One for the Gipper" halftime speech. The "Gipper" was George Gipp, Notre Dame's first-ever All-American football player, who died of throat cancer on December 14, 1920, just days after leading the team to a victory over Northwestern.

Although my father never became a Notre Dame hero, he was able to use his Notre Dame education to become a legend back home in upstate New York. He graduated with degrees in history and English, the first in his family to graduate from college, fulfilling both his and his own father's dream. But he wasn't done yet.

He returned to New York and went to Albany Law School. Back then, lawyers were viewed with far greater respect, even awe, than they are today. They were trusted, viewed as pillars of their communities. It was a real privilege to become an attorney.

I can only begin to imagine how proud my grandfather must have been. Just half a century after my great-grandfather had come to the United States seeking a better life for future generations of his family, my father aced it: the great-grandson of an immigrant managed to become a star athlete in high school, the backup quarterback on two of the most famous Notre Dame teams of all time, a graduate of a respected college, and a lawyer.

In 1933, he met and married my mother, Margaret Donahue, the daughter of a very well-known, respected, and established family in Albany. Dad's dynamic personality and character, his personal drive, and amazing story became linked with the backing of one of the region's most influential families to help chart his career trajectory: politics. It was a powerful combination. And I was the child to whom the expectation was passed—the attainment of education, business success, and political relationships became part of my DNA.

Dad launched his political career in the 1930s, an exceptional and transformational time in the history of the United States. Franklin Delano Roosevelt was president and the nation was in the midst of recovering from the Great Depression. Roosevelt drew generations of political lines in the sand by hugely expanding the role of the federal government in the lives of American people and institutions. He inspired the nation to jump on board the New Deal—a government-driven plan to get all Americans working again; American farms producing again, after the swirling clouds of the Dust Bowl that had afflicted the heartland; and American businesses building again, so that all Americans could benefit from the richness of this great nation. All this was accomplished during one of the worst economic crises in our nation's history.

Not everybody was keen on the New Deal. In fact, many people were affronted by FDR's tactics, viewing them as an entrée to socialism and the collapse of the capitalist, individualistic, personal-opportunity-driven world that my father's generation grew up in. Yet the history of these events serves as the basis for what I am today, something I never could have imagined, but the picture of what Dad envisioned for me, as his father had envisioned for him. My father built his own world and achieved personal success with the goal of pointing the way for his children.

FDR's vision was the foundation of the Democratic Party's philosophy and labor-grounded voting base. And while the area where my father lived in upstate New York was staunchly Republican, his head and heart were captured completely by FDR's political vision.

My parents settled in Rochester, one of the few Republican strongholds in the northern United States. That's where my father launched his political career as a Democrat, which was viewed as a foolish decision. The smart move, he was told, would have been to declare as a Republican, the dominant party in his district. It turned out that his party affiliation did not matter. My father's reputation and background were so strong that he was well known and respected among both Democrats and Republicans. He won his first election, becoming the assemblyman of his district, and served for a few years, during which my parents had their first child, my brother Don, in 1936.

Sometime in 1936, Dad decided to up the political ante and run for Congress. He was able to overcome the "stigma" of being a Democrat in a Republican area on the strength of his fascinating story locally, but it's much harder to cross party lines in a federal election because the district is often much larger and more diverse than the state legislative district. My dad was well known locally, and in the assemblyman state district, but many people in the district's other towns and cities did not know him. And when there is a lack of familiarity, voters are more prone to vote for a party than a person. Since the federal district was principally Republican, Dad's Democratic party affiliation resulted in a landslide vote against him—not because of who he was, but simply because he was a Democrat.

Not ready to give up on politics, he returned to the local scene and became public safety commissioner, which meant he was head of Rochester's police and fire departments. He also started his own one-man law practice. Even by today's standards, my father was a "good guy" lawyer, the kind that represented the underdogs of society—the lower class, the blue-collar workers, and the uneducated.

As I accompanied him to his downtown office, I saw how people would warmly greet my father. They often impressed upon me that I should be proud to be the son of such a successful and distinguished man. In the Boy Scouts and during our outdoor excursions, I saw he garnered the same respect. Everybody loved him.

I was my parents' second child, born in 1938, and my earliest memories of my father revolve around his work as public safety commissioner and as an attorney. As commissioner, he was provided a big black car with a little red light and siren on the top. He had his own driver, Bill McCann, a big Irishman with fists swollen from years of blue-collar labor and back-alley brawls. I loved driving in that car with my father; it was one of the most recognized vehicles in Rochester and everyone waved to us as we passed by.

But Dad didn't need the car to be recognized. Because of his political and legal work and sports legacy, my father was among the most respected men in town. No matter where we went in Rochester, people would rush over to him to shake his hand, tell him it was a pleasure to see him, and strike up a conversation about law, politics—local or national—or Notre Dame football, topics my father was always more than happy to discuss with anyone and everyone.

Whether I was in the car with my dad or by his side walking down the street, I felt special being with him. I walked around with my chest out and a proud "I am a Corbett!" attitude. It felt good to be the son of such a beloved man, a man the entire town looked up to because of who and what he was. He was a bona fide hero. While we were far from rich, we were well off. We had a three-bedroom home that comfortably fit our family. I was regularly taken on hunting trips with my father and a number of Rochester's most successful men. We went on weeks-long vacations to lake and beach homes. His children were dressed as the children of a successful attorney and politician should be dressed.

Rochester residents looked upon us as the picture of Americana, a family out of a Norman Rockwell painting. Little did they know that we had a secret we kept hidden from the world—we were far from perfect.

3

My Mom Was an Alcoholic, and I Struggled to Hide It

My mom's drinking became the thing that defined her, and it took me a very long time to learn that there was nothing I could do to change that.

My mother's family had a cottage on Saratoga Lake, a beautiful and picturesque vacation spot in upstate New York, and every summer we would take a month-long vacation there to swim, fish, hunt, water-ski, and go boating. Boxing champion Jack Dempsey and other celebrities would vacation on the lake. There was an elegant racetrack where well-to-do families decked out in the latest fashions would congregate for the big horse races. Saratoga Lake was the type of place that could fill most children's heads with a lifetime of happy memories.

Not mine. Instead, even today the lake elicits sad and even dark memories.

Like the time in my teens when my parents and us children were packed into our car, luggage strapped to the roof, headed to the lake. Mom was particularly drunk that day, sipping a glass of Four Roses whiskey and ginger—her favorite drink—and rambling on and on. I cannot remember what she said that finally set my father off, but I will never forget his reaction.

He swerved off the road and slammed on the brakes, sending dirt into the air and covering everything with a spray of dust. Staring straight ahead, his hands never leaving the steering wheel, he addressed my mother in that angry yet matter-of-fact tone he used whenever he was particularly frustrated or bothered. "Peg, we have all had enough of your drinking," he said. "It needs to end." Her response was to take another sip of her drink. My father's calm demeanor dissipated, giving way to his fury. He got out of the car, slamming his door so hard that the car shook. He stalked to the other side of the car, opened my mother's door, and demanded that she get out.

I don't know why she obeyed. Perhaps she was afraid. In truth, she had no reason to be. My father may have looked angry, but he had never once in his life laid a hand on my mother or even threatened her with physical harm. Perhaps she thought my father wanted to talk to her out of earshot from the children. Or perhaps she knew what my father was thinking of doing and she wanted to see if he was bluffing.

When she got out, my father, without saying a word, slammed her door shut, stalked back to the driver's side, climbed back into the car, and drove off—leaving my mother behind.

He had called her bluff.

My brother and I, though both teenagers, had the same reaction as my younger siblings—we started crying. In between tears, we begged my father to stop the car, screaming that he couldn't leave Mom behind and that surely she would change her ways and stop drinking. Finally, after driving a little more than a half mile, he slammed on the brakes again, swung the car around, and drove back toward where she stood. I'll never know if he did so because of our cries or because he never planned on leaving her there in the first place; I would like to believe the latter.

Dad pulled up next to Mom. He did not get out to open the door for her. He didn't even look in her direction. She stood outside the car for a few moments, a little embarrassed, I would guess, probably wondering how she would face her children. Finally, she got into the car and we drove off, with no one saying a word for the rest of the trip to the lake and tension filling every second of the drive. I still remember how angry I was on that drive. I was angry at my mother for her uncontrollable drinking. And I was angry at my father for leaving her behind, even if it was only for a few moments. Everything else in our lives seemed so perfect—and I could not understand why this dark family secret had to ruin things.

When we finally made it to the lake house, the first thing my mother did was mix herself a fresh drink.

In time, my mother drank herself to death. I was only 19 when she died. She never got to witness my success in college, politics, graduate school, or business. She never met my wife or had the opportunity to enjoy being a grandmother. She cheated herself out of so much, and I guess she cheated me as well. Sometimes I wonder if she ever really knew us, and I wonder if I ever really knew her.

Since the deeply sad day of her death, whenever I've celebrated a milestone in my life, no matter how happy I am, at some point a bitter sadness pokes me in the side, making me wonder why she couldn't have been there with me to celebrate. I wonder again why she did it, why a bright, attractive, well-educated woman had to poison herself. Why was she so unhappy? And how did her drinking affect my life? Who would I be today if my mother had been a June Cleaver rather than a Miss Hannigan, the villain who made Orphan Annie's life so hopeless?

* * *

My mother was born Margaret "Peggy" Donahue, one of six siblings raised in Albany, New York. I don't have many memories of her father. He was like a baron, sitting in his comfortable chair in the Saratoga lake house, smoking a pipe, and expecting all his grandchildren to treat him with the greatest respect. I know he made his living as a well-known insurance broker, and I know that he was a forward thinker for his time, as evidenced by his sending my mother to college in the 1930s, when supporting a daughter in pursuing higher education was not the norm.

She attended Cornell University and, according to her friends, was one of the most beloved people on campus. She was outgoing, the type of person who lights up a room upon entering, always making a grand entrance like a Broadway actress bursting through the curtains to applause. With her personality, background, and budding education, she probably could have excelled in anything she wanted to do. But in 1932, late in her freshman year at Cornell, she met my father, who was in law school at the time. She never returned for her sophomore year, leaving school to marry him and start a family.

Our first home was on Ridge Road in Rochester; later we moved to a larger house in a more upscale neighborhood on Browncroft Boulevard. I have few memories of our home on Ridge Road, but I vividly remember Browncroft Boulevard, where I spent most of my childhood and teenage years.

It was a two-story gray house with a large attic and red tile roof. Concrete steps led up to the front door, and we had a basketball hoop in the backyard and several big red beech trees that I would climb in the front yard. The bedrooms were on the second floor, the master on one side and two small bedrooms on the other. My older brother and I each had our own room for a few years, but as a boy I think I spent more time sleeping next to my mother than in my own bed. She was cuddly then, before the alcoholism corroded her spirit. When the family expanded to five siblings, my brother and I moved into the third-floor attic, which we converted into a shared bedroom.

Directly behind Browncroft Boulevard was Corwin Road, where the more well-to-do neighbors lived. Around the corner was Winton Road, home to a small business district that included a gas station, a barbershop, a bakery, a drugstore, and a small ice cream shop called Scoops, where my brother and I both worked as teenagers.

My best friends—aside from my older brother—were the two Hammond boys, who lived directly across the street, and the Schollanberger boy, who lived on Corwin Road. We would play baseball in the street or shoot hoops in my backyard. Or we would play in the small creek and open fields at the end of Browncroft Boulevard, building campsites and pretending to be cowboys in the Wild West.

I attended Catholic grade school at St. John the Evangelist. All the teachers were nuns and the school was run by Father Sullivan, an old Irish disciplinarian who with one stern look put the fear of God in every young boy who dared get out of line. The school was only a 10-minute drive away. During the cold fall and winter, my mother dropped us off. When the springtime weather arrived, my brother and I would either walk to school or ride our bikes.

Whenever I returned from school or elsewhere, I would generally find my mother passed out somewhere in the house—fully inebriated. Home alone all day, she would drink. I believe that being "alone" played a deadly role in my mom's life. In fact, my very first memory of my mother revolves around her being alone. We were still living on Ridge Road and I was in my playpen, banging on the rails and screaming that I wanted my father. I remember my mother telling me, "Your father is not home. Your father is never home."

Because of my father's work as both attorney and politician, he was on the road a lot, traveling four, five, even six days a week, back and forth between Rochester and Albany, leaving my mother to tend to the home and children by herself. Dad was around enough to teach me to play football, hunt, and do the other things fathers pass on to their sons, but he was not there to be part of the daily routines of raising us. I think my mother was often overwhelmed and lonely.

Perhaps that's why she drank. As a young woman, the world was at her feet. But she left it all behind for my father. And then he left her alone to manage the raising of five children. Perhaps she was depressed about how her life turned out. Or perhaps she had been a victim of the disease of alcoholism and drank only because she was compelled by her genetic makeup.

When I was a child, I did not care why Mom drank, but I sure spent a lot of time hiding her from the world. She was an embarrassment. She would often be too drunk to make it to the store to buy whiskey, so she would call Charlie, the local grocer, and ask him to deliver it—a service that his store offered to all its regulars. When I was in grade school, I hated getting home from school and hearing a knock on the door, because I knew it was probably Charlie bringing my mother more poison. My mom would usually be passed out on the couch in the living room or upstairs in her bedroom, so I would rush to the door before she woke, not because I wanted to tell Charlie to go home—she would get the liquor sooner or later—but because I did not want Charlie to see the state my mother was in or the state our house was in.

Charlie knew Mom was an alcoholic, but I fantasized that if I could keep her hidden, he might forget. I would open the door only a crack, not wanting him to get a look inside. When I couldn't get to the door in time and the knocking woke her up, she would always force the door wide open. Staggering in place, wearing an open bathrobe covering stained pajamas, her hair a mess, she would greet Charlie with a giant, "Hello, Charlie! How are you?" her arms extended to the sides like a loving aunt exaggerating how big a hug she wants to give her favorite nephew. My mother was theatrical even when sober. When drunk, she took it to another level. She was a happy boozer, like the drunks Carol Burnett would mimic. When my mother was drunk, nothing bothered her. Life was good—for her.

Charlie would always smile politely when she came to the door, pretending he didn't know she was drunk. He would engage her in small talk, telling her that he and his family were doing just fine, thank you. Sometimes, she would invite him in, and I'd be horrified and I would whisper to Charlie, "Please, Charlie, don't come in." He got it, and would politely tell my mother that he couldn't come in because he had other deliveries to make. But sometimes she would grab him by the hand and drag him inside anyway, and I would go from embarrassed to humiliated.

Our home was always a mess. Dishes would pile up in the sink. Laundry was scattered everywhere. Sometimes household objects would be strewn across the floor. On really bad days, when Mom had spent hours drinking on the couch, jars filled with urine would be scattered on the floor because she would be too drunk to stagger to a bathroom. My older brother and I did our best to clean up when we got home from school, but Charlie would often arrive before we had time to clean. So when my mother tried to drag Charlie inside, I would always grab the liquor, put it on the counter and push him back out the door. I believed that if I shooed him away quickly enough, he would not see the mess. I had the illusion that I could protect myself from what other people already seemed to know.

My mother was our dirty little secret, the elephant in the room who we wanted to keep hidden from the world. My father was often invited to join country clubs but always had to turn down the offer because he knew mom would embarrass the family at the club. She was constantly embarrassing all of us.

Sometimes, when my friends and I would play basketball in my backyard, she would knock on the window and ask me in a slurred voice to come inside to help her with something, or to run to Charlie's grocery store to pick up dinner and a bottle—always a bottle. My friends stifled their laugher when she appeared in the window, disheveled and red-faced, but I could feel their ridicule and it burned me up. Other times my mother would stumble outside and watch us play for a few moments and then launch into an extended discourse, telling my friends embarrassing stories about me. It was impossible for my friends to contain their laughter during such instances, and they would sometimes point and hold their bellies as they laughed. I hated it. I suppose it was selfish to think of myself first, to think of the embarrassment I was suffering rather than the fact that she was slowly killing herself. But I was just a kid and that's how kids think.

As a teenager my attitude changed. I no longer had the luxury of thinking about just myself. I had to think of my two younger brothers and younger sister first. My father was away at work. Someone had to look after my siblings. On the many days my mother was too drunk to tend to the family, Don and I took up the task. We would stay up late cleaning, wake up early and prepare breakfast and lunch for my younger siblings, and then make sure they went to school, did their homework, and got good grades. Don and I were just kids ourselves, but we had to become the parents tending to the home that none of us had.

I began looking after my mother as well, trying my damnedest to get her to stop drinking. I went through a phase in which, when she would pass out, I would take every bottle of alcohol in the house and pour it down the drain. When she found out that I had emptied all her bottles, she would become furious with me and berate me for wasting money, but I would do it again a few days later. In time, I learned it was futile; it was an endless cycle—I would pour the liquor out and she would buy new booze the next day. I guess I could have demanded that the grocer stop selling her liquor, but I think that would have been futile as well; she would have found someone else from whom to get her fix.

I tried asking her to stop drinking. And when that didn't work, I yelled at her just as my father did, as if she was a child. Sometimes that worked, and she would stop for a short time, a few days or so. Then I would come home from school and find an empty bottle on the floor. I was defeated. I could not figure out how to get her to stop. Back then, alcoholism was not yet viewed as a disease and treatment centers were not the norm.

When I accepted that she could not be changed, I turned my attention to protecting her from herself. If I could not keep her from drinking herself to death, maybe I could at least keep her alive as long as possible. When I found her passed out facedown, I would turn her over. When I found her stumbling down the stairs, I would rush over to help her navigate the steps. It was breaking my heart, knowing that all I could do was try to keep her alive—for the time being.

Through it all, my father never seemed to cut down on his traveling. I understand that it was a part of his job, but I often wondered if he saw any connection between his being away from home and her drinking. Maybe his traveling so much wasn't just a matter of his job responsibilities; maybe he stayed away from home because he couldn't bear to watch his wife drink herself to death, and he felt there was nothing he could do.

But his continued traveling as she spiraled into a crash became a source of great animosity for me toward him. I realize now that he too tried to keep her from drinking. He too would dump out her liquor and demand she stop drinking, but to no avail. But I didn't see that then. I was just a kid and I believed, at the time, that he could have done more. As proud as I was to be seen with him when I was a little boy, I was equally angry with him when I was a teenager. Part of that anger may have been triggered by the burden of having to play a parental role at home because of his absence.

When I was a senior in high school, Mom was diagnosed with liver cancer. At that point, I had to give up hope of anything changing. The doctors said there was nothing they could do. She was dying. And I believe she knew it.

One Saturday morning her doctor, Howard Friedman, came to the house to take her to Strong Memorial Hospital for therapy. I welcomed him in and he called upstairs for my mother. She did not respond. He called a few more times, but still no response. I trekked upstairs to see what was taking her so long. I found her lying in bed. She did not have the strength or desire to go for treatment. She had lost the will to live. We had to force her to go. I called for my mother's best friends and neighbors, Edith Hammond and Sally Anderson, and they helped me dress her and carry her downstairs.

In 1956, I left home to attend Notre Dame. From time to time, my father would provide me with updates on my mother's health. They were never good. The last memory I have of spending time with my mother is the last time she visited me at Notre Dame. Mom and Dad came to the campus, spent the day with me and my older brother, Don, who was also attending Notre Dame, and we went to a football game together. I have a picture commemorating the weekend. She did not look healthy; her skin was yellow, which often happens when someone's liver is.wasting away. It was cold that day and she wore a mink. The photo was snapped right next to the Golden Dome after we walked out of St. Edward's Hall. Even if I did not have that photo to keep the memory fresh, I could never forget all that it captured.

A few days after my parents left campus, I visited the Notre Dame Grotto. I knelt before the statue of the Virgin Mary and tried to make a deal with her. I promised that if she saved my mother's life, I would be the church's servant for all of time. It didn't work. A few months later—in May 1957—my mother passed away.

Foolish as it now seems, after that I carried a grudge against the church for a very long time. I believed that God or the Virgin Mary could have saved my mother if they so pleased and when that didn't happen, I felt the church had turned its back on me. In response, I turned away from the church for many years. Eventually, I understood that my mother created her own death by her personal behavior and irresponsibility. It took living through other losses in my life to help me better understand that spirituality is helpful for all of us, even if I don't understand why cruel deaths are allowed.

On the day my mother was buried in Holy Sepulcher Cemetery in Rochester, a beautiful red northern flicker perched on a branch nearby. As my mom was lowered into the ground, the bird launched from its roost; the sound of its wings flickering into flight echoed through the silent cemetery. There was something symbolic about the noise, because as soon as I heard it, I felt a flicker in my heart, a sense of separation and grief that was very, very deep. Only years later, when my father died in 1996, and when my brothers died—Don in 2010, David in 2015, and Jim in 2016—did I feel anything so powerful again.

Following Mom's burial, I wanted to quit college; I had no desire to go back. My father wouldn't hear of it. He told me in his matter-of-fact tone that I would return to college. It was exam week when I got back on campus. The entire week is still a blur. I passed all my exams, but I have no idea how.

When the exams were complete and I had time to think about my mother's death, I was able to think differently about my father. I realized that he had done all he could to save my mother, but she did not want to be saved. And I saw how my mother's death affected him.

Dad stopped working for two years. He became a recluse, staying home almost 24 hours a day. And he went from being an absentee father to an overprotective one. He rarely let my two younger brothers and younger sister out of his sight and would not let them do anything that could be considered remotely dangerous. The man who had taught me to hunt decided it was too risky a sport for my younger brothers.

I think his overprotectiveness made us into a different family than the one that Don and I had experienced. People who knew us would say we seemed like two separate families—me and Don as the brothers in one family, and David, Kathleen, and Jim as the siblings in another. Obviously, my younger siblings were also severely affected by my mother's alcoholism, through fetal alcohol syndrome, which occurs when pregnant women drink and pass alcoholic poisons through their own bloodstreams to the babies in their wombs. It can result in a range of behavioral and even physical disabilities for the child. As I watched them grow up and into adulthood, I could see that my mother's drinking had affected their lives in many ways.

My mother's alcoholism affected me in a very different way and, in some ways, I think it contributed to my successes in life. First of all, it taught me the importance of wearing an emotional costume. By emotional costume, I mean I sought to appear externally optimistic and confident even though I nearly always felt the ripping apart of my heart and stomach. As a young person, I was busy trying to convince the world that everything was okay. I was always telling people, "Mom is great. The house is fine. Life is perfect. Our family is happy." Of course, the truth was Mom was not great, the house was a disaster, life was hard, and my family was falling apart. But I was so good at convincing people—except for the few who were able sneak past me into our home—that everything was great. Most of the town fell for it. I helped to keep the secret. Mom's alcoholism taught me how to bullshit. I became an expert at it.

As a businessman, I deployed these skills to my advantage. Early in my career, I was able to put on a nice suit and shoes, comb my hair perfectly, waltz into a bank, and convince the loan officer that I had a great portfolio and a can't-lose investment opportunity. I'd almost always wind up getting the loan. I had donned a costume of responsibility and it worked; indeed, this was the skill that launched my career.

My mother's alcoholism also made me independent. I raised myself. My father was simply not around to do it, though he did teach me to hunt and fish. My mother did not raise me, but she made it necessary for me to raise myself. I saw how dependent my mother had become on us, too. She needed Don and me to take care of the house and the younger children, she needed us to take care of her, and she needed us to keep her alcoholism a secret. I saw her dependency as a weakness. So I decided that I could count only on myself—and I was guarded in my relationship with others. That's the way business and much of the world work. It's a hard-knock life, and I found myself both literally and figuratively giving and getting some pretty good knocks in. All of that fueled my need to be my own man.

If Mom had been more nurturing, more engaged, more of a mother, maybe I wouldn't have enjoyed the success I have. Maybe I would have been another average guy. Perhaps if she had coddled me, I would not have had to mature so early in life and would not be the independent, strong-willed, often-irascible man I have become.

Still, a lifetime later, when I think about her, I feel a heaviness in my heart. I hope, and I guess I even pray, that Mom has somehow found peace and maybe even a happiness that I never saw her have in this life.

Despite all the booze, the embarrassment, and the mess that I grew up in, there were always occasions to escape. Outside the confines of the house, I had amazing and important opportunities to grow. These took me as far from my dysfunctional home as was possible—into the woods, streams, fields, and mountains of the outdoors, where I learned about hunting, fishing, surviving in the wilderness, and the role of leadership in groups.

CHAPTER 4

I Almost Ate a Boy Once

My father was always keen on exposing me to the wonders and challenges of outdoor life, including hunting, camping, and managing in the wild. When I was just 15 years old, he took me on my first deer-hunting trip with some of his friends—local lawyers, judges, and politicians. This was a tradition for these men; every year they went together on a deer hunt. The legal hunting age was 16, but no one on the trip was going to rat me out. In their minds, as long as I was Don's son and could handle a gun, I was old enough to hunt. And hunt I did.

One day, as I ran through the woods, I suddenly found myself in an open clearing staring at a magnificent eight-point deer. He had not yet seen me, so I silently crouched on one knee and instinctively took aim with my shotgun. I fired a slug. It exploded through the deer's shoulder and dropped him to the ground with a heavy thud. Shaking from the adrenaline rush, I sprinted over to the deer to finish him off. I was so excited that I did not think about the trophy his head could have provided and instead aimed at his head for my kill shot. I could not steady my hands, however. My slug missed his head and instead shattered his antler. The errant shot angered and now emboldened the deer. His shoulder wound gushing, he leapt to his feet. I was rattled and jumped back several feet. The wounded beast stared me up and down, lowered his head and charged! I had only one slug left. Without taking the time to aim, I fired.

To this day, I have no idea whether I hit him again or missed completely, but he kept coming and I was out of slugs. So I turned the shotgun into a bat. As the deer came upon me, I clobbered him on the head! He fell to the ground unconscious, where he finally bled to death from the shoulder wound.

My troubles were not over yet, though. I couldn't think of leaving such an extraordinary trophy behind, but I was over a mile from the cabin. I grabbed the deer by his one good antler and dragged him the entire way back, digging a new trail with the weight of his body against the ground as I went.

My father would later cover for me by tagging the deer as his own. When the game warden came by to check up on us, despite it being obvious that a skilled hunter such as my father would not have made such a messy kill, he took my father's word for it rather than scolding me for breaking the law. Boys will be boys.

A few months later, I was introduced to one of the great Boy Scout rites of passage: the Philmont Scout Ranch, a 214-square-mile rugged wilderness in the Sangre de Cristo range of the New Mexico Rocky Mountains and the largest national Boy Scout camp in the nation. Sangre de Cristo means Blood of Christ, an apt name as it turned out.

Today, Philmont is a dream come true for Boy Scouts looking for well-managed but challenging adventures. Activities include mountain climbing, swimming, burro racing, gold panning, horseback riding, mountain biking, rifle shooting, and backpacking along hundreds of miles of rough, rocky trails. It is well staffed and each adventure is well planned and safe.

But back in 1953, Philmont was more rugged and challenging than it was well managed. It was a seriously isolated wilderness. Boy Scouting was very much about survival skills. We were expected to learn what it took to survive on our own in the forest: how to establish a safe base camp, how to catch and prepare food on our own, how to find our way in uncharted forests, and lots more. We went on camping trips during the year in upstate New York, honing our skills along the way. The scouts from across the country who exhibited the most independence and the best survival skills were then selected to showcase their talents at Philmont on a survival weekend. I was one of them.

The idea of the survival weekend was to challenge us to survive in the wilderness on our own for four days—with no chaperone or adult intervention. Adults marched a group of four scouts dozens of miles across dangerous, remote terrain, leaving the marked trails behind, and left us perched in the middle of nowhere with only an axe, knife, tent, and a change of clothes. Before leaving, they gave us one directive: survive!

One guy in my group was called Piggy. He was chubby and squeaky, and he helped me learn what relative survival really meant.

After choosing a campsite, our first order of business was to clear the area and pitch our tent. We swept away the leaves, sticks, and rocks so that only the cool dirt lay under our tent. We then searched the area for any signs of snakes, scorpions, beehives, poison ivy and its relatives, and any other signs of danger. Once we established a safe campsite, we decided to find ourselves dinner. Plants and leaves were not an option; we needed meat or fish. But without a firearm or proper fishing pole, how would we find food?

Unlike that deer-hunting expedition with my dad's friends, at Philmont Scout Camp, we didn't have conventional hunting tools like a shotgun. But if we thought outside the box, as I had when I used my gun as a bat, we figured we could accomplish our goal. We started by chopping a branch off a tree, tying a vine to it, carving a hook out of another branch, digging for worms, and then using the contraption to fish. We were feeling pretty good about ourselves, bragging how easy the adventure was. We were soon proven *so* wrong.

We cast our line and waited, and waited, and waited, and waited, and waited some more. We sat on that riverbank from early afternoon until late at night and never felt one tug on that line. I pictured the fish laughing at us. "You think we're gonna be fooled by *that* hook?"

By the time we gave up fishing, it was too dark to light a fire and we didn't have a flashlight. The stars and moon provided us with light and the summer air was warm in New Mexico. Even with the howling western winds, we were able to survive the night without extra heat. When we woke up in the morning, though, our stomachs were growling, telling us that if we didn't come up with a new food-gathering tactic, we might not survive another day with our sanity and health intact.

Since fishing had not worked, we decided hunting would be our next plan of attack and that we would do so with our knife and axe. Philmont had plenty of animals to hunt—deer, rabbit, elk, buffalo, turkey. Though I had some experience with stealth hunting, I was neither stealthy nor quick enough to sneak up on an animal and spear it with a knife or slice it with an axe. The other three scouts were even less equipped. So we decided to hide behind trees, wait for an animal to walk by, and then throw our knife and axe at it.

The first animal that came by was a deer. *Jackpot,* we thought. The deer stopped in the middle of a clearing near where we were hiding. I had the axe in my hand and knew I was the stealthiest. So I motioned to the others that I would sneak over to the deer and do the deed. I quietly walked, undetected, to within 10 feet of the deer. Slowly I raised the axe. Then I thrust it forward as if hurling a baseball toward home plate. The axe flew true, but my aim was terrible. I missed the deer by a good two feet, and the sound of the axe crashing into ground sent the animal sprinting.

We reworked that strategy all day—hiding in the woods, throwing our knives, axes and even rocks at every animal that passed. Finally, just before the sun set, our stomachs were growling so loudly that a passing hunter might have mistaken us for bears. It was then that we caught our breakfast/lunch/dinner. Our team of superscouts, selected from across the country based on their proven outdoor prowess, finally worked successfully together to complete the hunt. We caught ourselves a chipmunk—one, small, measly chipmunk. The tiny animal stopped in a clearing, we all picked up giant rocks and in unison took aim on the chipmunk. I don't know which of us hit it, but one of us slammed a rock into the chipmunk's head, killing it instantly.

We carried our "haul" back to the campsite. It took three very frustrating hours of banging rocks together over a pile of dried leaves on top of small sticks to finally get our fire going, and we cooked our sumptuous meal. When we were done eating all that was possible to eat, we were still starving. A chipmunk does not have enough meat to feed four hungry teenage boys.

We felt defeated. We were tired and hungry. We had not eaten anything resembling a meal since breakfast the day before we hiked to our camping spot. We were beginning to learn part of the lesson of Philmont: real survival is hard. But we knew that we had to keep our focus in order to have any chance of making it. If we began to allow our minds to slip, we would be lost. The adults were not coming to get us for another two days. We were very much on our own with only each other to depend on.

As the second evening wore on, we found ourselves plagued with thoughts of food. And it was all Piggy's fault. He started talking about food and would not stop. If the idea of starving wasn't bad enough, Piggy spent the entire second night whining about the specific foods he missed—strawberries, hot fudge sundaes, candy bars, and so on. The more he spoke, the hungrier we all got and the crazier we became. We asked him to stop—but he wouldn't.

The next day was more of the same. We hunted all day and came up short again. Piggy continued to cry about food the entire time, driving us closer to the brink of something crazy. We still had another day and night to go before the adults came to get us and we did not think we would make it. We were really hungry—hungrier than any of us had ever imagined being before. It was affecting the way we thought as individuals, and then, as a group. Darkness, deeper than the night, came upon three of the four scouts.

That night, when Piggy literally cried himself to sleep, we crept outside the tent and hatched a plan. We were not going to starve. If we did not do something radical, we would die. We actually started joking that either we would die or that we might have to eat Piggy. We were not serious, but we needed a distraction from what seemed like a real survival problem. So while Piggy slept, we huddled together and contrived all manner of ways we might prepare Piggy and eat him. It was like telling ghost stories around a campfire. It made us laugh and it certainly killed time for a few hours.

Moments after discussing the plan outside the tent, we heard a loud rustling in the bushes nearby. We thought perhaps it was an animal—maybe an answer to our dinner prayers! We quietly motioned to one another to grab our weapons and prepare to attack. But before I could get my knife out, the predator leapt from the bushes.

It was our scout leaders. Apparently, they had never really left us alone. They had set up camp a mile or so away and at least one adult was looking in on us. They knew our frustration and failure to find food, and their job was not to starve us. They decided that our survival weekend was over.

The leaders hiked us back to civilization and got us a real meal. We all promised to never speak about dinner plans for Piggy again. But for many years, several of us, when together, would break a dull moment by quipping, "We could always eat Piggy!" And it never failed to bring a combination of laughter and groans.

While adults were protective back then, I believe I was afforded more flexibility and opportunity to be on my own. I brought a lot of natural and learned resourcefulness with me to that survival camp. I had the cool outdoor skills I'd learned from my father. And I'd learned about survival *inside* of our house as well—by becoming a caregiver for my mother and for my younger siblings when she was incapacitated. Being alone in the woods required physical survival skills. But being the lone caregiver out of necessity built emotional and interpersonal survival skills—skills that are essential in the cut-throat real estate business. My acquired toolbox of interpersonal dynamics included carefully navigating required political and social niceties; maintaining a fundamental distrust in everybody; and being able to read people and circumstances to optimize the compelling, driving need to make the deal work *for me*, and to feel good about it (meaning that I might relish having beaten somebody at their own game).

These turned out to make me a better hunter—both in the woods and in business.

CHAPTER 5

I Found a Mentor—and a Kindred Spirit

Always a leader, my father put together Rochester's first Cub and Boy Scout troops, an activity that would contribute substantially to my outdoor, survival, and leadership skills.

Dad approached Father Sullivan at St. John's with the idea, explaining that if the church provided the troops with a location and helped recruit leaders, he would oversee them in terms of paperwork and funding. Father Sullivan agreed that scouting troops would be a good activity for the young men in the community and suggested that Lou Langie become the scoutmaster.

Langie was the perfect role model for the young men in Rochester. He was in his twenties and could still relate to teenage scouts. He was also an ex-athlete who had excelled on the Princeton University boxing team. His family owned Langie Oil Company, one of the most profitable companies in Rochester. But Langie was not some hoity-toity guy. He was down to earth—more of a blue-collar man to the core—often choosing to get his hands dirty rather than work in the office. He loved the outdoors and possessed extensive knowledge on the topic. And, most important, he and I shared the privilege of having alcoholic mothers.

He never told me back then that his mother was an alcoholic. I didn't find out until some years later. But the fact that he had an alcoholic mother meant that he knew how to treat me. He had seen my home and met my mother. Whenever he came to my door to pick me up for a scouting activity, he never asked to come in and knew how to refuse my mother's request for him to do so. When he came by and my mother was particularly drunk, he knew exactly how to act so as to fool me into believing that he was unaware of her drinking problem. As far as I knew, he was oblivious to my mother's dirty little secret. But he must have seen some of himself in me.

Langie became a real mentor to me and encouraged my leadership skills. That was a big part of what Langie did—he provided mentorship to budding leaders.

I was always the junior leader among scouts, from the Cubs all the way to the Boy Scouts. When we went camping, I pitched the tents and led the scouts in starting a fire. When we went hiking, I took the lead. When we were in community parades, I carried either the Scout or US flag and did so boldly, looking like a leader should— chest out, shoulders square, with an air of confidence about me.

When I failed my Philmont survival weekend, I was ashamed of myself because I felt that I had let Langie down. Everyone back home thought I had the skills to survive. I felt that Langie, in particular, expected more of me. I returned to Rochester from Philmont embarrassed, but a year later I had another chance to impress Langie with my survival skills. Hell, almost the entire troop did.

By then I was 16 and our troop had mastered the rough waters in the Adirondack Mountains and its tough backcountry. We had spent a day in high rapids, level water canoeing, which helped prove our young teenage toughness. But Langie was all about building toughness with integrity. After canoeing, Langie took us to a local café, where we saw a very rugged, bearded outdoorsman take a knife and carve an aching tooth out of his own mouth, without exerting more than a muffled grunt. Wow, those locals were tough cookies! Langie wanted us to have more of a challenge and a new test for us to master.

Today parents would scream for Langie to be jailed for wanting to take us on so many dangerous missions. But I believe that's what separates our generations. We weren't coddled; we were allowed to scrape our knees, slip on river rocks, and experience other risks that prepared us for the physical and emotional challenges of adulthood, business and the responsibilities of family.

To test us, Langie and another scout leader took six of us Eagle Scouts to Chibougamau, a small town in Central Quebec, located on Lake Gilman, now famous for its hiking trails. Back then, however, it was so tiny and off the map that some of its waterways were barely charted. There were maps of the waterways we would travel down, but the maps were old; no one had bothered to update them for years. This was our ultimate test—we were going where few men had ever gone before us.

The plan was to hike for a few days, launch our canoes into the river, paddle downstream for a day or two, and then hike again. We would be traveling back to New York, where we had a car waiting to take us home. The entire trip was to take 10 days in terrible weather (since it rained for nine days). We had good fishing and caught more than 60 fish, including large northern pike between 15 and 25 pounds, and encountered a huge moose swimming across the lake.

However, the raw surroundings we were navigating were quite dangerous.

For the most part, our maps were accurate. I stress "for the most part." Many of the rapids were not marked and there was no indication as to whether the rapids should be portaged or shot.

According to our outdated map, the river up ahead was supposed to be still and tranquil. But the map was inaccurate. As we rounded a tight bend, our entire world was transformed into jagged, vicious rock-strewn rapids. There was no way out. The next few moments were a blur. The torrent of water overcame our ability to control the small canoes. My friend John Talmadge and I were able to help each other make it safely to shore, literally tugging our still intact canoe with us. Others didn't have it so easy.

We collapsed into the shore's mud, our lungs filled with more river water than air. When we stopped choking and looked back toward the river to see if everyone else was okay, we saw another canoe smashing against the rocks, breaking into dozens of pieces. I then saw the angry river toss my brother's canoe into the air. My brother and another scout leader flew out of the wreckage of the canoe. As their bodies were tossed into the river, a part of me feared that would be the last time I'd ever see my brother alive. When I saw Don's head bob above the rapids, I almost cried for joy. He and the other scout in his canoe made it safely to shore.

Fifteen minutes after the adventure began, we all lay in the mud by the river, happy to be alive. Born leader that he was, Langie did not allow us to celebrate our luck. He reminded us that while we had survived the river, we still had to make it back to civilization. This was not some campsite with a hotel and a Denny's a few miles away. There were no cell phones. We were in the middle of no man's land. We would have to rebuild the canoes if we were going to make it home; it was too far to hike.

Obeying Langie's orders, we collected the pieces of the canoes that made it to land and hiked a few miles down shore, looking for a safe place to set up camp and rebuild the canoes. We ended up stumbling upon a group of Cree Indians who made their living in the forest as lumberjacks. We were fortunate to be welcomed at the lumber camp by the senior lumberman and his staff.

The Cree had a bold and attractive appearance, but they were stoic—no smiles or laughter lightened their manner. The men we met were tall and slender, with not an ounce of fat on their bodies and every muscle rippling through their skin. They had long black hair and perfectly defined cheekbones. Even though I had met lots of hard-working men back in Rochester, I couldn't help noticing that the hands of these Cree men were huge from years of hard, outdoor labor. I was struck by their rugged confidence and that they seemed to fit so naturally and comfortably into this deep backwoods world. I remember thinking that there was something almost time-less about them, that the wild outdoors had more conformed to them than they had to it.

But there was also something unsettling about them. Remember, not only were we miles from even remotely modern conveniences, but we were in Canada—a foreign country—and they did not speak any English. They spoke a mixture of Creole and French, and it was clear they had not had much contact with outsiders like us. It was unclear if they were offering us help, telling us to go away, or talking among themselves about eating us. Langie came through again. His French was good enough to communicate, and they agreed to help us. We were told to follow them.

They led us, pieces of our canoes still in tow, a few more miles to their village, near the riverbank. Now, forget everything you think you know about Indian villages. I expected a bunch of teepees or thatch huts, but their village consisted of beautifully handcrafted log cabins. The Cree had cut down trees, chopped and carefully shaped the logs, stacked them, and sealed them together using mud or sap or some kind of cement-like substance. There was no electricity, no running water. But these were comfortable, safe, well-made living quarters where an entire community lived.

Few of the Cree met our eyes or otherwise engaged us. I guess the uncertainty about them scared most of us. We were really not sure what was going to happen. That night we slept in a cabin that belonged to a few Cree who apparently found someplace else to sleep for the duration of our stay. Adding to the uncertainty were the artic timber wolves native to that part of Canada. They howled all night and often sounded as if they were right outside our door.

It had been a rough day. We had nearly drowned in the rapids. We had hauled heavy, broken canoes and what little gear we could salvage for miles through rough backwoods. And now here we found ourselves, tired and confused, in the middle of a remote Cree village and sleeping in one of their cabins.

I don't remember sleeping much at all.

The next morning, Langie got us up and organized, then led us to the long house, a cabin that stretched to the size of about 10 residential cabins. It was their communal facility lined with long tables, where the Cree lumberjacks were already eating breakfast when we arrived. We sat near the end of one of the tables, feeling slightly awkward as well as guilty about dining on these hardworking souls' food. I was the last of our troop to sit down. Two very large, strong Cree men and one young man sat down next to me at the very end of the table, saying nothing.

Breakfast was pancakes, served on plates, stacked high and passed down the long tables. The largest and strongest of the Cree men, who probably did the hardest work, took and ate the most—three to four pancakes apiece. The older and younger men dined on one or two. As the plates with hotcakes came down the table, each of the scouts took just one pancake, not wanting to abuse our welcome. But just being in the village, and especially in the long hall, created a situation.

When a plate was passed to me, I quietly removed one pancake. Four remained on the plate as I carefully passed it to the enormous, unsmiling man next to me. I figured more would be served. Three Cree lumberjacks sat next to me. As it turned out, the cook did not account for the addition of a bunch of teenage boy scouts for breakfast and had not made enough to go around.

The Cree man directly next to me happened to be one of the largest and strongest men in the room. Without hesitating, he took three of the remaining four pancakes and slapped them on his plate. That meant at best, the last two men would have to share one pancake. The next lumberjack, who was rather young, took the final pancake. The last guy, a mature man with huge hands calloused from years of work and fingers crooked from breaks and fractures, was not about to go without breakfast. As the younger man was about to eat his pancake, the older, larger man picked up his own fork and stabbed it into the back of the younger man's hand. Blood spurted everywhere, and every member of our troop gasped. *The savagery,* I thought and could not help but imagine that we were next, that the tribe was going to turn on us for taking their food. I contemplated the prospect of being slaughtered.

The young man who was stabbed barely reacted. Sure, he winced in pain from the stab, but he did not howl or cry. He simply moved his hand away from the pancake, allowing his older, stronger attacker to appropriate the breakfast. The young man then covered his wound and sat silently at the table, accepting the fact that he had been bested and would have to go hungry until lunch. In fact, none of the Cree men in the long house reacted; they didn't even shoot us an angry glance.

After breakfast the villagers provided us with wood we could use to repair our canoes. It took us all day. We spent one more nervous night in the cabins and then put our canoes in the river at daybreak the next morning. Thanks were offered to those who listened, but there were no formalities or niceties shared. A few days of event-free hiking and canoeing later, we were safely back in civilization.

The Cree men lived in a world where survival was far more primal than anything I had known or imagined. Each day was quite literally a struggle to get food, protect the village, and get enough rest to go back to work the next day. This struggle was normal for the Cree. That they did not turn on us confused me for some time. But over the years I came to understand that they were treating us as the lost guests we were. They had no issue with us personally and had no need to cause us any harm. They probably wanted us out of there as much as we wanted to be out.

As I grew older and was able to put that trip into perspective, my view changed. I was the guy who, when backed into a survival corner, had once contemplated eating another human being after just two days of hunger pangs. Who was I to judge men who live deep in the woods, men who work harder in one day than I probably have in my entire life, and who have only themselves to depend on for survival, with no stores or restaurants to run to for food.

Looking back on my failed survival weekend and at the weekend I spent in the Cree village, I realized that *survival* is a relative term. For some, it's about having air-conditioning to keep cool in the summer; for others, it's literally about whether there will be any food for breakfast or if they will make it down the river without losing their boat and maybe their lives. I learned that the survival instinct, whether in the deep Canadian woods or on the streets of New York, was something that drove me to perform even if it brought out a bit of the natural savage in me.

I came to believe that even if somebody was part of my inner tribe, he might stab me with a fork if I threatened something that was important to him. When it comes to survival, defined in relative terms of the next pancake—or the next dollar—people will behave selfishly and even viciously. My fundamental distrust of others grew out of this understanding of how people behave when things important to them are threatened or when they really want something. Even some family members or best friends might just take out that fork and use it on me.

I learned that persistence and really hard work are the most important keys to success in anything, especially survival. Sure, luck and good reactions play a role, but mentors like Langie encouraged me to never underestimate what I could do and to never forget that the strong and the clever will find a way to survive, even if it's at another's expense. So I was going to be stronger and cleverer while learning to balance my own persistence, hard work, and reliance on the skills and expectations of those around me.

Life's challenging, painful, and glorious moments appeared more and more to me as something of a skillful dance, a responsive, reactive, calculated, and often distrustful set of interactions with other people—all of whom wanted the prize. Not everybody is going to play nicely or even fairly. I also had to remember that sometimes I could get the pancake, and sometimes the fork. So I had to learn to fight—but in a civilized, acceptable way. No forks or guns, just brains and wit, combined with seasoned brawn—knowing how and when to defend what I had—and how and when to attack to get what I wanted through controlled aggression.

That was a skill I mastered in the boxing ring.

6

I Love Punching a Man in the Face

There is something deeply exhilarating about the perfect fit of a man's cheekbone against your fist. That perfect fit, when timed just right, is followed by an elegant, quick click of his head snapping back, his knees buckling, and his will to stand on his own wilting—all in a split second. Over and over again, I reveled in the abject superiority of outmaneuvering, overpowering, and outthinking another man in the boxing ring. It infused me with a rush of confidence and a desire for more.

I had to find my own path. I had lived in the shadow of my mother's alcoholism and had always been second to my big brother, Don, in nearly everything. I had not been my own guy and knew that I needed something to set me apart. That something became clear when I was 12 years old.

Lou Langie, who had been a member of Princeton University's boxing team, announced to our scout patrol that he wanted to teach the scouts how to box. When he asked for a show of hands from those interested, my hand was the first one in the air. Boxing would mean it would always be just me and my opponent in that ring. Win or lose, it would be on my shoulders, not Don's. It sounded like the perfect way for me to earn my own name in town. As I looked around at the other volunteers, I saw a hand belonging to a tall, skinny, sandy-blond-haired boy raised high above the rest—it was Don's. No matter, I thought. I didn't care whether Don boxed or was better at it than me. All that mattered was that I'd have the opportunity to stand on my own.

Eight of us took Langie up on his offer, and the following day we began our training at the local Catholic Youth Organization (CYO).

The CYO was housed in a three-story building with fading yellow bricks located in a low-income area of Rochester. It smelled of sweat all the time. Even freshly cleaned, it smelled like sweat overpowered by Pine-Sol. The first floor had a basketball court where local church teams had a league. On weeknights, the teams practiced. On Sundays they played hotly contested games. On weekdays and on Saturdays throughout the fall and winter, the court was always busy with pickup games, as Rochester's best street ballplayers flooded the gym to escape the bitter cold and play on a court not covered in ice and snow.

The third floor had a track for running and a room full of what we'd now consider archaic running machines. The treadmills were made of rubber curtains laid atop wooden spools, with no motors; the faster you ran, the faster the spools spun. The timers had to be wound up by hand and they looked like egg timers. And the exercise bikes were rusty outdoor bikes placed on cinderblocks.

The second floor was my second home. That was where we boxed. One end of the second floor contained a musty locker room and showers. The other end had a weight room, offering only free weights, no fancy machinery or weights tied to cables. If you wanted to get big and strong, you bolted iron weights to a bar and lifted. In the middle of the second floor was a giant open space containing a boxing ring, wrestling mats thrown on the floor to provide more area for sparring, a space for jumping rope and shadow boxing, and an area where heavy and speed bags hung.

The CYO was always clean and well kept, but it was a far cry from the country-club-type fitness facilities most people work out in today. The CYO was a gym, through and through. It was a place where young boys molded their bodies into rock-hard fitness and became men. Our CYO was old school. And so was our training.

Langie taught us footwork, combinations, head movement, and every other skill a boxer needs to survive in the ring, but the most important lesson he taught us was how to be tough. When we sparred, he never matched us up against someone in our own weight class; he matched us up with someone multiple weight classes above us. I was tiny when I started my training, a paperweight at 105 pounds. But Langie would put me in the ring with a handsome French kid named Joe Rabideau, a welterweight and an experienced fighter who weighed about 140 pounds. Joe was more than just heavier than me; he was much taller and had longer arm length. He would work his jab against me—at Langie's insistence—forcing me to learn ways to get inside. Once I did, he would lean on me, wear me out, and destroy me with an uppercut if he connected. Before I figured out how to fight him, he broke my nose three times. I would have to slip his jab, duck inside, quickly deliver a three-punch and a two-punch combo in succession, and then dance away from him, avoiding his clinch on the inside and his jab on the way out. It took my best footwork and timing—the stuff of boxing.

Unfortunately for my face, on more occasions than I would have liked, Joe's jab would be too crisp for me to avoid. I would have to absorb two blows, shuck them off, and then slip inside so I could do my damage. I just had to hope I could land blunter blows than Joe's and inflict more damage. Though it was a brutal strategy, it worked and it taught me how to take a punch and move forward as though I'd never been touched. That strategy alone turned out to be an important life experience. In business and my personal life, I found myself getting hit all the time, sometimes intentionally, sometimes just because of the circumstances. The ability to take the punch and move forward, which Langie forced me to master, set me up to be resilient and to focus on the goal.

When I wasn't sparring, Langie worked on essentials with me. He would have me charge, bobbing and weaving, toward the heavy bag as though it was Joe, and deliver my combos—left jab, left jab, left jab—and once they landed I would deliver a right cross and a left jab, then dance away. He would clock the speed of my attack and each week he'd hound me to cut more time off my flurry; even the tiniest fraction of a second, he would howl, could be the difference between being knocked out and knocking out my opponent.

But the first big knockout of my life did not occur in a ring. It happened in the street. And it shaped an important part of me. I'd been training under Langie's guidance for almost a year. I was about 15 years old, and I probably weighed 125 pounds. It was winter, late afternoon, and it was cold. Snow covered the sidewalks and the streets were paved with the dark sludge that forms when cars drive over fresh snow, melt it, and stain it with exhaust.

I had just finished boxing practice. My friend Mickey Wade and I had been hitting the bags and practicing combinations that day. My muscles were still warm and loose, and my muscle memory was still fresh. The purpose of long, repetitive workouts is to punch as naturally as you breathe. To throw hundreds of combinations for a straight two hours, perfecting your style, strength, and accuracy, so that arms and fists behave in a disciplined, nearly choreographed way—but as if by second nature—so that you can concentrate on the mental demands of the sport.

Mickey was a 160-pound street fighter, a tough kid who had worked hard to become gym-trained as well. As the two of us left the gym, which was located in a rough section of Rochester, we felt stronger and tougher than anybody else on the block. As it turned out, we were tougher than six "anybodies."

We were only a few feet outside the gym when six teenagers rushed us. They started harassing us, laughing and taunting, mocking us for thinking we could fight just because we trained at a gym, and boasting how each of them could whoop either of us easily. I remember feeling intimidated. I didn't like that feeling. Between their street-tough looks and street-tough talk, they had a good bark. But the lesson I learned on the street that cold afternoon helped me realize I could do more than stare down the dog.

Mickey did not wait for their bite. He engaged them almost without hesitation, throwing a cracking left hook into the face of the nearest boy, leaving him on the ground and unconscious. Instinctively, I immediately followed suit and introduced one of the thugs to the three-punch and two-punch combos I had spent that day mastering—a left jab, left jab, and then another left jab, followed by a right cross and another left jab. *Bam, bam, bam! Whack!* The combos worked against a skull as well as they did against a punching mitt, and my overmatched opponent was sent crashing into the icy soot covering the road. A third thug tried to sucker punch me from the blind side, but I sensed it coming, ducked and then finished him off with the same combo.

I stood poised, waiting for the next fool to come near me, but no one else stepped up. No doubt my impressive boxing abilities had something to do with keeping them at bay, but it was also because Mickey was a damned animal. He combined his well-honed and disciplined boxing skills with street aggression and savvy. He had already grabbed another of the teens, picked him up, and slammed him into a snow bank that lined a block of ice. He repeated the act and each time the boy's body hit the ice, it made a blunt thudding noise. I remember it as the sound that life makes when it's literally being slammed out of someone's body. The remaining attackers were shocked by Mickey's savagery; they wanted to help their friend, but they were too scared to move. Their bark had been cut out, and they were now watching the visceral bite of Mickey's remorseless pummeling.

Someone had to stop Mickey. He looked maniacal, as if he might kill the kid. I was concerned about getting too close, because in his rage, he might mistake me for an attacker. So I yelled to him from a few feet away, "Mickey, stop! You're going to kill him! Stop!" I repeated my plea over and over again, at least a dozen times and for at least three more slams, before he finally stopped, his victim looking like a bloodied crash test dummy.

When Mickey turned to face the two remaining frightened antagonists, they sprinted away faster than the Road Runner. If this had been an episode of *Looney Tunes*, smoke would have shot from their trail in the snow.

With three teens beaten into the soot and the snow bank, Mickey and I headed down the road. Actually, we strutted away, in a *this-is-my-town* walk. The streets and the town were ours.

I'm not one of those old guys who lectures his grandchildren that fighting is terrible and that true men have the courage to walk away from a fight rather than engage in one. There are times in life when a man is challenged to defend himself with his fists. Facing up to that challenge is a test that has real value.

Let me clarify that I mean testing yourself with your fists—and only your fists. Fighting with weapons is for sissies. Win or lose, you'll never know more about who you are as a man than when you battle another man with only your God-given brains, brawn, and athletic ability. Even if you lose, you learn something positive about yourself. You may be bested in the fight, but at least you had the courage to stand up for yourself. Even a loss can give you self-confidence, as well as awareness about your weak spots.

Langie's training tactics worked. Because everyone on the team learned the same technique in the same manner, we were the best boxing team in the area. Two years after our training began, in our first team competition—the Mission Bouts—we won every weight class we entered, and I brought home the bantamweight title in an epic fight. The Mission Bouts are a tradition in Rochester, more than 80 years old. Sponsored by the Aquinas Institute—the Catholic high school I attended—every year since 1930, it's the tournament that determines the best boxers in upstate New York.

My Mission Bouts took place over several weeks, and each of us had to defeat four to five opponents along the way in order to be crowned champion. Thousands of people packed the downtown civic center for these fights. They filled the center with smoke from cigarettes and smelly cigars. They guzzled beer. They cursed at the kids fighting. They gambled. It was quite a scene—and quite intimidating. Our headgear was made of thin leather, the type football players wore in the old days, not the thickly padded headgear that amateurs wear today. With such minimal head protection, knockouts were more common than they are in amateur bouts today.

I easily beat all my opponents in the bouts leading up to my championship encounter. They were all so much lighter than the opponents I fought in practice that I felt like I was fighting little kids, not teenagers my own size. For the championship bout, I was matched up against a kid named Johnny Canaan, the winner of two previous Mission Bout titles in different weight classes. He was two years older than me and a lot more experienced, a tough street kid who had never lost a fight either inside or outside the ring. I was the underdog, but I believed I was better.

I proved it in the first round, dominating him with my quick feet and three-punch and two-punch combos. But he took charge of the second round, pummeling me time and again with a vicious left hook that I could not stop. With just seconds to go in the round, he connected with that hook yet again, this time sending me tumbling to the mat. Carmine Basilio, a former middleweight world boxing champion, was the special guest referee for the fight and administered the count. It was the first time I'd ever been knocked down; that shocked me as much as the punch. I was bloodied and battered. I could see Basilio's hand gestures making the count, but I couldn't hear a word he said. Finally, I was snapped back into reality by the sound of the bell ending the round. At the count of six, I was literally saved by the bell.

I knelt in the middle of the ring on one knee, still dazed, my eyes glazed over, trying to locate my corner, and a tiny elderly Italian woman with an accent that was half old-country and half New York began banging her umbrella on the ground, yelling at me, "Get up, you little bastard! I bet on you! Get up!" I wanted to yell back, "Why don't you come in here and fight this guy?" That's when I felt a pair of cold hands grab me around my waist and pull me to my feet. It was Langie dragging me to my corner.

He tossed me onto the stool and my brother Don hurried over to douse me with a bucket of ice water. It was a dramatic, chilling bath, but it woke me only momentarily. Don slapped me across the face, telling me to snap out of it or I was going to lose. That didn't work either. Langie tried to give me instructions, but it was useless. I couldn't understand what he was telling me. My eyes were open, but my mind had shut off. I was punch-drunk.

Basilio pushed his way through my corner to inform me that I had 15 seconds to go before the third round. I felt disoriented and unfocused. I didn't want to go back out, something I'd never felt before. But I knew I had to finish the fight. I preferred a knockout loss to a forfeit.

I stood up and prepared for my execution. Don pushed himself into my face—this was as important to him as it was to me. He knew what I was feeling and he reoriented me sharply, looking me squarely in the face, yelling, "Left hook! Left hook! Left hook! Left hook! Look out for the left hook! Look out for his left hook! It's all he has!" He grabbed my right arm, put it against my own head and instructed me, "You keep this arm up! Keep this arm up! Keep this arm up, dammit!" Then he gave me a light shove toward the center of the ring.

Looking at my opponent across the ring, I was scared shitless. The bell rang and he came darting toward me, wanting to end the fight quickly. He wound up for his left hook. "Left hook!" Don yelled from ringside. "Put up your right arm!" I did. And I blocked the punch.

Canaan was shocked but would not give up. He began wildly throwing that left hook, as I blocked it each time, gaining more and more confidence with each blow I deflected. I saw that my brother was right. The left hook was his only weapon. As long as I was mindful of it, he couldn't hurt me. I went on to dominate the third round and won the fight and the championship by decision. Don helped me focus on what I needed to do. He helped me keep my eye on the prize and keep my wits about me even in the most dazed state.

I competed in the Mission Bouts three more years, winning titles in the next two and losing the championship by decision in my fourth and final tournament. There was a reason for the loss, however. I had not slept the night before, tending to my mother as the cancer ate her body. After that experience, I considered trying out for the Bengal Bouts boxing competitions in college, but doctors discouraged me. My nose had already been broken four times and I had a deviated septum.

Besides, my face was ugly enough already.

The lessons I learned from fighting are still fresh in my mind, especially the importance of the role my brother played in that first win of the Mission Bouts title. I wanted to box to get out from Don's shadow, yet it was his aggressive intervention that helped me to win the fight. The lesson I learned was about my pride. There are some things I would need to do alone, but I would learn to rely on others to help me get what I wanted. I could not allow my pride to be my greatest enemy.

Boxing also taught me about strategy. It taught me how to be an aggressor with a defensive mind. Size and stature can be overcome. I learned never to back down from anyone. I would always push forward but temper my moves to ensure that I didn't charge forward blindly. I learned to be aware of my opponent's best weapon and to be prepared to stop my attack momentarily to defend against it.

Most important, I learned that meaningful successes are not easily achieved. Anyone can feel confident when things are going right, but how will you react when someone punches you in the jaw, literally or figuratively? Will you stay down on the canvas and give up, or get back on your feet? Life is filled with surprises, and it's always challenging. But the sport of boxing can teach us something about hard work, survival, and what it takes to get back in the ring.

CHAPTER 7

I Am a Workaholic

For as far back as I can remember, I have been working—often to the exclusion of other things in my life. Work offered a distraction, if not an antidote, to weakness and dependency.

My mother's dependence weighed me down like an anchor. Dependence made her weak and I resolved at an early age that I would never allow myself to appear weak; nor would I allow myself to be dependent on others. I didn't want to take even one penny from my own father. I paid for everything myself. I wanted to be my own man.

By the age of 12, I already had multiple jobs. I'd wake up before the sun rose every morning to deliver newspapers. I delivered to around 60 homes in a five-block neighborhood. The money was not great, but the job taught me responsibility and the value of money, and it allowed me to purchase such goodies as ice cream, cookies, and candy. While most of my friends could enjoy these treats only once every few weeks, I could do so every week if I wanted.

My second job also helped me to satisfy my sweet tooth. I worked at Scoops, the local ice cream shop. What a terrific job. I was paid well and was allowed to eat all the ice cream I could fit in my belly— without having to pay for it! I can still remember the prices: single dips were 5 cents, double dips were 10 cents, and hot fudge sundaes were 20 cents.

As my body filled out and my athleticism and strength developed, I turned to blue-collar, hard-labor jobs. My love of sweets was replaced by a love of sweat. Once I discovered boxing, I became obsessed with becoming the toughest kid in town and working hard-labor jobs provided me with a way to build my body while earning a paycheck. One summer I worked loading 100-pound, 4-inch-thick 4-by-4-foot bags of concrete onto trucks for a construction company owned by John Bianchi, an old, hardened Italian contractor from Rochester. Within a month of starting the job, I had developed the legs of a power lifter. You could spend years in a gym squatting every plate on the rack and still not get the type of workout that carrying cement bags provides. Men with blue-collar muscle are always stronger than those with gym muscle.

Late that summer, though, the regular workers went on strike, leaving only the part-time help and the strikebreakers to handle the entire workload. I was promoted from bag carrier to cement truck driver. I was just 16 years old, had my license only a few months, and had zero experience driving large trucks. During my second or third day as a driver, I was behind the wheel of a flat rear bed truck loaded with 100-pound bags of Portland cement. As I drove down a rut-filled dirt road leading to the construction site for a home, I was feeling pretty confident … until the truck hit a huge hole, tossing me into the air. I felt the truck shift to the right as I tried to hang onto the steering wheel and next thing I know, it was on its side.

I quickly climbed out of the window and was trying to get my bearings when fear seized me about what just happened. Some of the Italian workers ran over and after they saw I was okay, they started laughing. They decided they'd better help me out before I got fired and they'd have even more work to do. They teamed together to push the multiton truck back upright. Only a few dents were noticeable and they put me right back in the driver's seat.

That episode reinforced for me the truth of another old adage: If you fall down, get right back up and do it again. Persistence—learning that I could overcome short-term failures of all kinds—was a lesson I learned early on. Whether I was facing the painful daily frustrations and disappointments at home with my mother, or getting back in the ring after being knocked down by a left hook, or, later on, handling the initial defeats handed out by zoning boards or city councils regarding land use, I always responded the same way: getting back up, regrouping, and not taking "no" for an answer. Getting back in the ring or into the truck became a matter of instinct. But I also learned that I could often rely upon others, friends and family, who might help me get back up and into the good fight.

Lou Langie, my boxing coach and Boy Scout leader, also provided me with opportunities to earn money. If I needed extra cash, I would go over to his company and perform whatever job he needed done that day. All the members of our boxing team were welcome to do the same. Some days we'd wash the company trucks; other days we'd shovel coal. As we matured, he gave us opportunities to make "real money" as salesmen.

Coal-burning stoves were giving way to oil burners at that time, and Langie's family's company was one of the first to try to make a buck off the new technology. Our job was to go door-to-door and sell people on switching from coal stoves to oil burners to heat their homes. Our sales pitch was, "Not only is oil cleaner than ever as a fuel, but it will keep your home cleaner. You will no longer have barrels of ash to throw away!" If I sold one oil burner, I would have enough cash in my pocket to take the rest of the week off. Sometimes I would, but more often than not I would continue working for Langie or one of several other employers. I was finding myself obsessed not so much with the money but with the idea of success—material success. I was doing something that resulted in tangible, recognized results, and money became one of the measures of that success.

I even worked while on vacation, and played just as hard.

One of the rewards my father's legal and political career brought to the family was a beautiful two-story waterfront cottage with its own dock on Conesus Lake, in the Finger Lakes region of upstate New York. My father did pro bono work for the Sisters of Nazareth, who owned the cottage. To repay him for the work he'd done for them and others, they provided us use of the cottage from June through September, whenever we pleased. It was ours for four months a year, and we would stay there off and on as my father's work schedule allowed. My memory of the cottage and the lake area remains one of pure beauty accented with an unlimited number of wonderful things to do—hiking, mountain biking and climbing, swimming, canoeing, and deep lake fishing.

We would often catch black bass and yellow perch off the dock. The fishing was easy and the catches made for great lunches, dinners—and sometimes breakfasts! One night, using large minnows as bait, we set a rod up with a rock weight attached and left it overnight. The next morning, my bobber was underwater and somehow the rock weight had kept the pole on shore. I rushed to the pole and began to reel in my catch. A large northern pike leapt out of the water, my hook in its mouth. It was the biggest fish I'd ever had on a line, and I was not about to let it get away. I fought it for a good half hour before it gave up and decided to become my trophy. It was a beautiful fish—almost a yard long. A neighbor heard of my feat and took a photograph of me holding the catch, which looked almost as tall as me in the picture, and I made the front page of *The Genesee News*, the local newspaper. I can still recall the thrill I had reading the story and the pride my dad expressed having his son on the front page.

Don and I found a job in a cornfield about a mile from the lake cottage. We would wake before the roosters every morning and jog to the field. After all the corn was harvested, the cut grass was bailed into hay that had to be hauled and loaded into trucks. That's what Don and I did. And the work was not for the meek.

During the summer, when you're working outside in an open field, bailing and harvesting, the heat is magnified. Out in the sun, sweat coated my skin from head to toe. Hay is brittle and can have sharp points, and the pieces come in all sizes, from hunks to microscopic. The hay would stick into me like darts—all over my body, inside my socks and shoes, in my hair and my ears—causing lacerations that would swell and get sore. We tried wearing jeans and long sleeve shirts, but it was just too darn hot. The best way to sling hay bales was to do it in shorts, without a shirt. The cuts and rashes were better than heat exhaustion. Hauling hay was the most miserable job I've ever had, but Don and I never shirked our responsibilities. We didn't take lots of breaks or try to avoid the heavy lifting. It was uncomfortable, even painful, but we saw it as a responsibility we had agreed to take on, and both of us had already learned and embraced the work ethic that came down from our father's father and his father.

The coolest job I had as a youth was one I created myself. I started a photography business. The first time I used my Brownie camera was magical for me. The Brownie was created and sold by Eastman Kodak, whose headquarters was in Rochester. The Brownie was one of the first handheld cameras designed for popular use. It changed the photography industry. Just as the digital video camera has allowed everyone on the street to try his hand at filmmaking, the Brownie allowed anyone to capture life in photographs.

I purchased my first camera with my own hard-earned money and took classes at a weekend photography school sponsored by Kodak. The school taught me how to use the camera and develop the photos. The artistry, though, I had to figure out for myself.

I practiced every day. I photographed friends and family, wild-life and nature, and street scenes. I turned part of our basement into a darkroom, and it became my favorite place in the house. No matter how many photos I developed, I was always amazed by the magic of the piece of shiny, blank paper slowly flickering alive with silver dots to form a perfect, real-life picture of somebody looking back at me.

As my passion for the camera grew, so too did my obsession with success and entrepreneurship. While attending a dance during my sophomore year in high school, the idea came to me to start my own photography business. The school had always employed a profes-sional photographer—a grown man—to capture the school's happy couples on film. I remember standing back and watching dozens of couples standing in line, having their pictures taken, and paying the man $4 in cash for a single photograph. Most couples bought more than one copy. It was a cash machine. And I could not help but ask myself, "Why can't I be the dance photographer?"

Throughout the next week at school, I worked my angles, walking the hallways promoting the fact that I, Dick Corbett, would now be offering less-expensive, high-quality photographs at the next dance. I was already something of a big shot on campus. And though it may sound arrogant, my reputation was well earned. I rarely got lower than an A-minus in any class, was known as a tough kid because of my boxing skills and I was a good all-around athlete. I had already established myself politically—I was a class representative freshman through senior years, having drawn on the natural political skills inherited from my father. Because of my reputation, I think students would have come to me for photographs, even if mine hadn't been cheaper than the regular photographer's. But my photos were a full 50 cents less for each one and I offered deals on multiples, which the regular photographer did not offer. I played to the market and to my strengths. The regular photographer never stood a chance com-peting against me, once I decided to enter the field. I was a blatant opportunist—and loving the entire process.

I called my enterprise Campus Color. Don would hustle around the dance and drum up business, while I would snap the photos. We charged $3.50 per photo and our overhead was only 20 cents each. We were photographing up to 200 couples a dance, selling each cou-ple multiples, and the school held one or two dances a month. We earned ourselves one hell of a profit. Combined with what we made from all the other jobs we worked, our earnings were enough to pay our tuition at Notre Dame.

In later years, I recall feeling a degree of guilt about taking work away from the local photographer—a man who was likely feeding his family with the money he earned. But that guilt gave way to the pride I enjoyed in having built a successful venture. I had become independent, and would never let go of that. I loved the way it felt and I wanted more.

CHAPTER 8

I Became a Part of History

Like Forrest Gump, I seem to land myself in historic situations and alongside historic people. But that doesn't happen entirely by accident. The largest stumbling block between a man and success is fear—fear of failure, fear of humiliation, fear of putting everything on the line and losing it. It's much easier to live safely, never take a chance, and live out the average life. Those who choose that path never experience colossal failure or humiliation, but I also don't think they're ever fully alive. If you want to experience life to its fullest and accomplish all your dreams, you have to get rid of that fear.

I am not sure why, but I was never held back by fear of failure or humiliation. I was always confident, always willing to take chances, always willing to do everything I needed to succeed. And I think that's what propelled me to the top of my class at Notre Dame.

The first time I stepped foot onto Notre Dame's campus I knew I had arrived at a time in life that would position me for the future. I saw that big, beautiful golden dome, the gorgeous brick buildings dating back to the 1800s, and the beautiful, bright, upper-class students everywhere. And I knew that this school would offer me everything I needed to succeed in life in whatever field I chose. I was also realistic enough to understand that the opportunities were not going to be hand-delivered to me.

Because of my father's status as a Notre Dame football alum, my brother Don was able to become friends with many of the Fighting Irish football team and reestablish the Corbett name on campus. The men on the team were the most popular on campus and being close with them meant you were popular by association. Thanks to my father and Don, when I arrived on campus, the team immediately accepted me as a friend as well.

One of the most important friends I had on the football team was Paul Hornung, the 1956 Heisman Trophy winner, whom the press nicknamed "The Golden Boy." Hornung played halfback, safety, and quarterback, and he could run, block, tackle, catch, and throw. Some still consider him to be the greatest all-around football player in Notre Dame football history. He was the biggest man on campus and just being seen with him turned me into a big man on campus as well.

I met Paul through my close friend Tim Ryan, now known for his work as a sportscaster, providing commentary for numerous historic sporting events—the Muhammad Ali–versus–Joe Frazier fight, the Sugar Ray Leonard–versus–Marvelous Marvin Hagler fight, three Stanley Cup playoffs, three Winter Olympics, and 19 US Open tennis championships. In college, Tim was a well-loved student-media personality who covered the games. He never played football, but he was just as well known as the players. Our friendship also contributed to my popularity.

Still, it takes more than popular friends to rise to the top at Notre Dame. My ticket to the top was politics. Raised by a politician, I was drawn to other politicians; it was in my blood. I had become a politician in high school and planned to pursue politics in college. Freshman year was tough for me because of my mother's death. I made a concerted effort to make plenty of friends and get in with the right people that year, but I didn't assert myself as a campus leader. I had to mourn the loss of my mother before I could get back to establishing myself. When I returned to school for sophomore year, I was ready to make a name for myself on campus, ready to be more than the kid who was friends with the football team. I ran for class representative that year and won. My brother helped me run my campaign. He put up signs and knew which parts of campus had the most foot traffic at specific times of the day and where to stump for votes. The football team endorsed my candidacy, which was the most valuable endorsement on campus.

The following year I became junior class representative, and the next year I became president of the Notre Dame senior class. Although my ties with the football team continued to be an asset, perhaps my most important asset was my relationship with Reverend Theodore Martin Hesburgh. Father Hesburgh served as president of the university for 35 years, 1952–1987, the longest tenure in Notre Dame's history. Under his watch, Notre Dame ceased to be known only as a football school and became a school known for top-flight academics as well. The numbers for endowments, research grants, enrollment, student population, faculty members, and degrees awarded annually all skyrocketed while he was president. He also served as a member of the United States Civil Rights Commission in 1957 and later chaired it in 1969. He served on a number of government commissions, nonprofit boards of directors, and Vatican missions. He was an amazing man, an exceptional leader, who became a friend and mentor.

Father Hesburgh told the student body that he had an open-door policy for anyone who needed his guidance. The majority of the students never took advantage of the opportunity to talk with such an accomplished man. I believe most students were afraid to knock on his door, afraid he would shoo them away or act as if he were too busy to be bothered by their presence. I wasn't afraid, and I wasn't going to pass up such an opportunity. He came to know me well and Father Hesburgh's name was a powerful one to have in my corner.

To run my senior campaign, I had one of the greatest political strategists of all time, a fellow student named John Sears. Sears wanted to become a campaign manager after graduation and later realized that dream working for two US presidents. Because of my popularity and my natural political leadership abilities, he saw me as the best candidate. He wanted a political victory on his resume before he graduated, so he approached me about running my campaign. His ambitions for his future rivaled mine and I knew that with him running my campaign, it would not suffer from a lack of work ethic. Too many years have passed for me to remember what my platform was, but the student body loved it and I was elected in a landslide. I give a lot of credit to Sears. He was good.

Unfortunately, Sears also taught me about the dark side of politics. As the election approached and it was evident that I was going to win, he grew jealous of my popularity. He told anyone who would listen that he should be president since I was only doing and saying what he told me to do and say. People repeated his comments to me, of course. He called me his puppet, which could not have been further from the truth. We were a team. I had the personality and vision; he had the know-how to spread my vision throughout campus. We complemented each other.

Years later, Sears fulfilled his dream and became a presidential election campaign manager, helping both Richard Nixon and Ronald Reagan gain the White House. However, Sears's ego continued to be his Achilles heel throughout his career. Reagan fired Sears during the 1980 election, claiming that the political strategist was overstepping his boundaries and trying to impose his will on others. In 2000, Sears's name again made national headlines when he was incorrectly identified as "Deep Throat" in Leonard Garment's book *In Search of Deep Throat.* Though we had our problems, I consider myself fortunate to have worked with such a talented political strategist so early in his career. Without his support, I might not have become senior class president. And if I hadn't become senior class president, I'm not sure what path my career would have taken.

Being president provided me with contacts most college students could never have. Throughout my senior year, I was regularly meeting world leaders. The first was Richard Nixon, who was vice president at the time of his visit, early in the first semester of 1959. To say that I was unimpressed with him would be an understatement. He was rude, arrogant, and uncaring.

It was my duty to present any visiting dignitary with an award. I presented Nixon with the Patriot of the Year Award. Yes, I'm well aware of the irony. I presented it at a celebration in front of the Morris Inn, the on-campus motel. Following the presentation, I was given the opportunity to have a one-on-one conversation with the vice president in one of the meeting rooms.

Nixon asked me what I was studying, reminded me to continue to work hard, and told me how lucky I was to have the opportunity to attend such a prestigious school. The whole exchange felt awkward. He seemed uncomfortable around me and our talk seemed more like a lecture than a conversation, but he was the vice president, so I sat back, answered his questions cordially, and soaked in the experience. I was 22 years old and talking with the vice president of the United States! It was surreal.

When Nixon was done with his sermon, I thanked him for the advice and promised that I'd continue to work hard. Just then, Herb Klein, his aide, tapped him on the shoulder and whispered something I couldn't hear. Nixon was never good at keeping secrets, and I heard what he loudly whispered back to Klein. "Get rid of this kid," he said. "I've got every local politician here to talk with me and I only have a few minutes left, so get rid of him."

In that moment, I went from feeling like the most important student at Notre Dame to feeling like a complete nobody. It taught me that no matter how important we think we are, we're only one sentence away from feeling like a failure. The ego is a fragile thing.

But my mother's alcoholism had taught me to cover up my emotions, my deep feeling of disappointment and almost shame. And as the boxing ring had instructed, even when you get hit hard, you move back and sort of smile it off. You have to create that exterior for your opponent in the ring. So I never let on that I'd heard and I didn't let it get to me. I wasn't going to let even a bad experience with a world leader stifle my ambitions.

Shortly after the Nixon visit, our campus began preparing for the presidential primaries. To assure high voter turnout among students, we held mock presidential conventions. Each candidate from each party was represented by a different group of students who campaigned for their candidate on campus. At the end of the campaign, the registered Democrats and the registered Republicans voted in their respective mock primary. Winners were then announced at a mock convention, and Notre Dame released a statement announcing which Democrat and Republican presidential candidate the student body endorsed. Notre Dame was such a powerful national presence that I suspect it had some effect on the election. Having the Notre Dame student body endorsement was a nice feather in a candidate's cap.

Most of the liberal Democrats on campus supported Adlai Stevenson, who was the one most respected in terms of intellect and Senate experience. All the political junkies and intellectuals on campus believed he was the most qualified candidate for the job. I decided to back John F. Kennedy. He was young, aggressive, athletic, bold, and fearless—everything that I thought made a great leader. I was in charge of his campus campaign. I organized get-togethers for his supporters, was in charge of signage and literature distribution, and spoke at events around campus about why the student body needed to support JFK.

Harris Wofford Jr., who went on to become a senator in Pennsylvania in the 1990s, was a professor at Notre Dame and was also part of JFK's national staff. He knew that the Notre Dame student body endorsement carried some political weight and arranged for JFK to visit Notre Dame in February 1960, while he was campaigning in the neighboring state of Wisconsin for the primary. When I heard the news, I promised myself that I would meet JFK.

I asked Professor Wofford if he could arrange it. He told me he would try to introduce me, but he couldn't promise anything. Father Hesburgh gave me the same answer. That was not good enough for me. I needed a guarantee that I'd meet JFK, so I took it upon myself to make it happen.

By then, I had become a JFK junkie, reading everything I could get my hands on about him. That's how I learned about Robert Sargent Shriver, best known as "Sarge." Sarge is one of the most impressive men I've ever known. He was JFK's brother-in-law, having married his sister, Eunice Kennedy. When JFK became president, Sarge used his connection to the Kennedy family to found the Peace Corps. Later, under LBJ, he founded the Job Corps, Head Start, and, with Eunice, the Special Olympics.

During the presidential primary, he was a campaign coordinator for the Wisconsin and West Virginia primaries. More important, he had become one of JFK's closest confidants. I figured if there was any man who could guarantee me a meeting with the presidential candidate, it was Sarge. I learned that he spent most of his time in the JFK campaign's Chicago office, so I tracked down the number and called.

I knew I had to make myself sound important if I was going to get him on the phone. When his assistant, Mary Ann Orlando, asked who I was, I said I was president of the Notre Dame senior class and close friends with Father Hesburgh and Professor Wofford, exaggerating the extent of my relationship just a tad. Moments later, Sarge was on the phone. I again explained who I was and stated (I didn't ask) in a very confident tone, "I would like to schedule a meeting with Senator Kennedy when he visits Notre Dame." And he said, "Absolutely." Upon hearing that beautiful word, I began shaking and sweating with excitement. I couldn't believe my phone call had worked!

JFK came to campus, gave a speech to a packed auditorium, took a tour of campus, sat down with the university's leaders, and met with me. I did not spend much time with him—probably 15 minutes at most—but those 15 minutes were enough. He was everything Nixon was not. He spoke *with* me, not *at* me. Nixon seemed uncomfortable with me, whereas JFK was naturally at ease. Though JFK asked me the same questions that Nixon had posed, the exchange didn't feel like small talk. It was two people having a conversation. He seemed genuinely interested in what I was studying and what my future plans were, and he appreciated my efforts to support his campaign on campus. Before our meeting adjourned, he told me to call Sarge after I graduated and ask about a job. I was flying high! Not only had I met my political hero, he had offered me a job!

In spite of our heroic campaign efforts, JFK lost the Notre Dame mock convention. Stevenson won the endorsement.

I graduated in June of 1960 with a double major in English and history. Before the graduation ceremony, I presented a plaque to a visiting dignitary—Dwight D. Eisenhower, the president of the United States. What a moment! I then headed over to the graduation ceremony, addressed the class, and introduced yet another dignitary—our commencement speaker, Giovanni Battista Enrico Antonio Maria Montini, later to be known as Pope Paul VI. Following graduation, I spent a few moments with him, but I couldn't speak Italian and his English was bad, so it was more of a "pleased to meet you and congratulations" moment. What a day! I met two legendary men in the span of 24 hours.

A few days later I took JFK up on his offer. I called Sarge to ask about work. He told me he was too busy to talk but would call me back. One day became two. Two turned to a week, then a few weeks, and I still hadn't heard from him. The chance to help with a presidential campaign was a big deal, especially when the candidate I backed was vying to become the first-ever Catholic and the youngest president ever. If he won, it would be an historic moment and I wanted to be a part of it. Unwilling to give up, I called Sarge one more time. I got through to him in the Chicago office, and reminded him who I was and of our previous conversation. "I'm going to L.A. for the convention," he said. "Meet me there. I'll find work for you on the convention floor."

Just like that, my career with the Kennedy family began.

The 1960 Democratic National Convention was held in the Los Angeles Memorial Sports Arena, one of the most remarkable sites I've ever seen. People filled the arena, from the floor to the rafters. The cheering was deafening and the energy was like nothing I'd ever felt before. You could drink 20 pots of coffee in 20 minutes and still not experience the rush that flowed through that arena. Everyone who addressed the crowd spoke with hope for America's future, banging the pulpit and screaming every word so loudly that even if the speakers had broken, the people at the top of the arena would have heard them. And in reply, the thousands in attendance cheered every word from every speaker, every decibel of noise thundering in the coliseum.

I was a floor runner for JFK, responsible for a block of states. My job was to run to each state's station, ask the chairman of the delegation how many votes his state had and who they were nominating, and bring my tabulations back to the JFK campaign. The Democratic Party itself had runners as well, but each candidate had his own runners to double check the party's numbers. With no computers or cell phones, that's how it was done.

I spent a hectic night zooming through the masses on the floor, bumping shoulders, and tripping over dozens of people. Before long I was covered head to toe with bruises, but it was all worth it. I got a firsthand look at history and was the first to know how some of the states were voting. As the night wore on, it became increasingly evident that JFK was going to be the Democratic presidential candidate. This was great news for me, not only because he was my political idol but also because it meant that I would be working for a presidential campaign.

By late evening, JFK still needed one more state to seal the primary. Wyoming, among my block of states, was about to announce its nomination. I knew Wyoming was nominating JFK, which meant its announcement would be the biggest moment of the convention. I rushed over to Wyoming's station to witness the announcement and got close enough to rub shoulders with Ted Kennedy. In a national news photograph, I was pictured next to Ted, who held up a Wyoming sign as the state's vote put his brother "Jack" over the top to win the Democratic presidential nomination.

Some people would argue that it was just luck that put me in that photo, but I didn't meet JFK by luck, and I didn't get the floor runner's job by luck. I took the bull by the horns and controlled my fate. I didn't let fate control me.

Like Forrest Gump, my brushes with history were far from over.

9

One of My Saddest Days: When JFK Was Inaugurated

My work for JFK's campaign earned me prime seats for his inauguration, only a few rows deep and in the center. Snow blanketed Washington, DC, that day and bitter winds burned every inch of exposed skin. The ice made roads dangerous and sidewalks deadly. None of that mattered. Jack Frost at his worst couldn't keep the Kennedy fans away from the historic event. JFK was the first Catholic president and the youngest president ever elected, and he brought a level of contagious excitement to the nation. I'd been drawn to him for his youth, aggressiveness, athleticism, boldness, and fearlessness, and now those strengths had won him the election. Of course, his looks, his dynamic family, and his beautiful wife were powerful assets as well. The inauguration was the first day of the Camelot reign and everyone wanted to attend.

People would have paid whatever price I asked for my tickets, but to me they were priceless. I had six tickets in all. My guests were my family: my father; my older brother, Don; my younger brothers, David and Jim; and my sister, Kathleen. The event is as fresh in my mind today as it was when it happened. Like so many Americans, I can recite portions of JFK's inauguration speech in my sleep:

> We dare not forget today that we are the heirs … that the torch has been passed to a new generation of Americans—born in this century, tempered by war …

The last few lines were the most memorable and compelling voiced by any president in US history: "Ask not what your country can do for you—ask what you can do for your country." They captured the theme of JFK's presidency. World War II had ended only a decade and a half before, yet I believe the younger generation may have forgotten that a nation thrives because its people are willing to make great sacrifices. Those lines reminded the entire nation of that fact and inspired a generation to make the necessary sacrifices to continue to move forward. It was one of the most historic moments in the history of this great country, and I had earned VIP seats to witness it firsthand.

But witnessing JFK's speech is not my fondest memory of the inauguration. I was especially moved seeing Joe Kennedy beam with pride over the accomplishments of his son. The older Kennedy was born in Boston to immigrant parents with little to their name. As odd as it now sounds, Boston was a place that discriminated against Irish Catholics when Joe Kennedy was a boy. He was raised at a time when Irish Catholics were treated as second-class citizens solely because of their nationality and religion. I learned later that many people had told Joe that he was a nothing, a loser. But he did not allow discrimination to get the better of him. Instead, he used it as a motivator. He wanted to prove them wrong by becoming a success. He attended Harvard and went on to become a multi-millionaire through the stock market, commodities, and real estate ventures. No matter how successful he became, he never forgot his early days of harassment, so one can imagine the pride he felt the day his son became the most powerful man in the free world, proving that Irish Catholics were the equal of anyone in the country.

JFK sat on a platform in front of the White House, watching the inauguration parade drive by, as people paid their respects to the new president, as is the tradition. No one paid more respect to the country's new leader that day than JFK's father. As Joe Kennedy cruised by in a white convertible, he motioned to the driver to stop in front of his son's platform. The driver obliged and Joe stood up, his white tie blowing in the wind, and tipped his black top hat to his son, the president. It was a simple gesture with a powerful meaning—he was proud of his son. I looked over to JFK to see his reaction. He was smiling from ear to ear like a little boy soaking in his father's congratulations after getting the first base hit of his baseball career.

Isn't that what it all comes down to for many of us? No matter your age, if you were raised properly, all the money, all the fame, all the friends, none of it makes you feel as good as your parents telling you they're proud of you.

I recognized that same look in my father's eyes that day. He could not believe what I had accomplished. His son, at the young age of 22, had already risen to a level of success that allowed the family to sit front and center for one of the most important presidential inaugurations in the history of the United States. When I saw the pride he felt, my heart swelled. But I wished my mother were there to share the occasion with us. I wished she, too, could have beamed with pride, and that's what made it one of the saddest days of my life.

Following the inauguration, my family and I went back to our hotel rooms. As my father and I sat silently in mine, both contemplating all we had seen that day, I looked out the window and saw some World War II veterans walking by the hotel a few floors below. Seeing them reminded me of a trip to DC that I'd taken years before with my family, when we watched the Memorial Day Parade together and marveled at the accomplishments of our veterans. That had been an important moment in my life because it laid the groundwork for my interest in this country's leadership and politics. My mother was key in my memory of that first trip to DC. It was before her alcoholism had taken hold and she was by my side the whole time. I was just a boy, enjoying the company and attention of his mother. Staring down at the street and experiencing the memory of her was painful. I missed her as much then as I did on the day she was laid to rest.

My long silence caught my father's attention and he walked over to the window to see what I was looking at. Once he saw the veterans, he did not need to ask what was going through my mind. The veterans, coupled with my silence and my expression, were all the information he needed. He touched my shoulder and said, "Dick, I cannot believe we're here. This is terrific. Your mom would be proud."

I look back on that experience and recognize that it also held some irony. My seats to the inauguration were another example of how my mother's alcoholism benefited me: learning to wear a costume to mask my emotions was paying off. It had served me well as I became associated with the Kennedy organization.

A few months earlier, following JFK's Democratic presidential nomination, Sarge Shriver had offered me a job working for the presidential campaign. He was impressed with the boldness I displayed when I called him for a job after college graduation. He told me I was the type of man the campaign needed on its team. Of course, I accepted. People were begging for paying jobs on the JFK campaign.

I pictured myself jet-setting across the country with JFK, giving him advice on how to run his campaign, sharing all of the worldly experience I had garnered while running for office at Notre Dame. Well, maybe it would be more "propeller-setting" than jet-setting because *Caroline,* the Kennedy's plane, was a propeller aircraft.

Still, I imagined slipping into dozens of election-trail photos, as I would surely be by JFK's side at all times. And I imagined the campaign job leading to a high-profile position in JFK's administration.

The rude awakening came even before I got off the phone with Sarge. I would not be working on the glamorous campaign trail; he was hiring me to sort mail in JFK's Washington, DC, headquarters.

The mailroom was in a dark, dank basement that smelled of mildew and mold. It was the worst possible campaign job available. But I didn't allow the disappointment to get me down. I knew there were thousands of people throughout the nation who would have murdered me for the chance to have a paying job on JFK's campaign team. It was an opportunity. The jobsite was no mansion, but at least it was in the mansion's pool house. I figured if I worked hard, I would be invited to the mansion.

I was right.

A month or so into the election, David Hackett, head of the campaign's mail, visited the mailroom. Hackett was a fascinating man— handsome, athletic, and he talked a mile a minute. My guess is he had what is now known as extreme attention-deficit disorder. He was also one of the most confident men I've ever met, which made him a natural leader. If Hackett told a roomful of people to jump into a lake, they would do so without asking why. There was something about him that made people want to follow, no doubt hoping that doing so would enable them to get to know him. Among the many people who fell in love with him was author John Knowles, who based the character "Phineas" from his classic *A Separate Peace* on Hackett.

Hackett had been a prep school buddy of Bobby Kennedy's. That was the pattern in JFK's campaign team: not only were most of his top advisors as handsome, athletic, and charismatic as he was— which helped create that tidal wave of energy flooding the nation, they were also his childhood friends. He never doubted their trust and loyalty. When they told him something, he believed them. So we all knew that getting on Hackett's good side could launch our political careers. If Hackett told JFK that one of us could help the campaign, he'd believe him. And that's exactly why Hackett was in the mailroom that day. He was looking for someone to serve the campaign as its Midwest coordinator.

The person named to the position would be in charge of dispersing election material to 17 states. A regional coordinator's job was like that of a shopkeeper or a warehouse foreman. He had to make sure each city and state office had enough signs, shirts, bumper stickers, and so on, and stay on top of the manufacturers of the supplies, the distribution, and so on. He also had to make sure each office had enough volunteers. If it didn't, it was his job to find another city or state office with too many volunteers and send some to the office in need. Finally, the regional coordinator had to ensure that JFK's political propaganda was dispersed when and where needed. For instance, if a specific city's major issue was civil rights, the coordinator had to ensure that all of the campaign's publications on civil rights were sent to that city and distributed to the correct media outlets and community organizations. It was a *big* job.

Why did Hackett think he'd find the right candidate in the mailroom? Simple. Everyone in the nation wanted to work for the JFK campaign, which meant even the lowliest of positions, such as those in the mailroom, were filled with Ivy League graduates. Everyone with whom I worked was my age and had resumes on a par with my own. They were all the best and brightest at their schools and were all qualified for the job Hackett was looking to fill.

Hackett explained what the position entailed and asked for a show of hands from those interested. There were a dozen young men in the room and a dozen hands shot into the air, a dozen voices raised, each trying to scream louder than the others, desperately trying to state his case as to why he deserved the job. I won out for one reason: I was the best bullshitter in the room. I knew how to wear that emotional costume better than anyone there. I told Hackett that I had gone to Notre Dame, so the Midwest was like a second home to me. And having been senior class president, I had a book of connections as thick as an unabridged encyclopedia.

It was all a lie. I rarely left campus when I was at Notre Dame. I knew next to nothing about the Midwest. And while I did get to meet an impressive list of world leaders as senior president, none of them were about to take my calls. Hell, there was hardly anyone in the entire Midwest who knew who I was! The truth didn't matter, though. Hackett bought everything I said, and I was named the Midwest coordinator. A few days later, I was shipped off to Chicago to begin my new job, working out of an office in the Kennedys' world-famous Merchandise Mart, then the largest building in the world—and a building that has its own story. I'll save that for later.

I may have grossly exaggerated my connections to get the position, but I was more than qualified and lived up to the challenge. Under my watch, no office ever lacked the proper campaign materials it needed. It was a simple case of being well organized and understanding each office's needs. I worked 20 hours a day, sleeping only from 2 a.m. to 6 a.m. The opportunity the job presented was too great to screw up. I would have worked 24 hours a day if my body had allowed me to. I was gaining valuable experience that would look great on my resume, and I was making invaluable contacts in the process. For instance, I was on a first-name basis with Senator Hubert Humphrey, an ardent supporter of JFK. He and his staff regularly called me to order more supplies for Minnesota's campaign office, and he always insisted that I call him Hubert.

Though Humphrey later became vice president of the United States, the most important relationship I forged was with Sarge Shriver. He was in charge of all of the Midwest operations and my position fell directly under him. Shriver was far different from most of JFK's buddies. Of course, he was handsome, athletic, and a born leader like the rest, but he was also an academic, a bookworm.

He lived by a different standard, too. Some of JFK's friends working for the election used their high positions in the campaign as a pickup line. Late-night election meetings often took place in bars and ended in strange beds as the sun rose the next morning. Shriver was never a part of such activities. He had strong Roman Catholic beliefs and was deeply in love with his wife, JFK's sister Eunice. These convictions meant he rarely cared to enjoy the nightlife; he was always at the Chicago office working on the campaign. And I was also always there working on the campaign, which allowed us to grow close. We spent hours talking about the election, and he schooled me on the history of the Kennedy family, specifically Joe—explaining how Joe's brilliant business mind paved the way for Jack's success. The more I learned about Joe Kennedy, the more I wanted to learn about him, and the more I wanted to be like him.

When JFK won the election, many of his campaign workers were worried about whether or not they would be offered jobs in the administration. I never worried. I knew Shriver would take care of me. Throughout the campaign, he repeatedly told me how impressed he was with my abilities and my work ethic. Shriver was not the type of man who tossed compliments anyone's way. If he said he was impressed with you, he meant it. Having his support not only helped me to obtain the impressive inauguration tickets; it also meant I was guaranteed a job in JFK's administration. I was hired as part of the transition team.

Before a president-elect takes office, he puts together a transition team. The team's job is exactly as it sounds: they ensure an orderly transition from the outgoing president to the president-elect. One of the jobs of the transition team is to review hundreds of agencies and programs in the federal government and select new personnel to manage these important offices. I was only 22 years old, but my job was to catalogue the positions in each agency and program and cull employment applications according to the specific jobs they were qualified to fill. Afterward, those above me weeded through the applications I passed along until each position was filled. The task was overwhelming because of the numerous positions available in each of the few hundred agencies and programs and because of the extreme number of applications we received. Everyone wanted to work for the Kennedy presidency.

JFK's enthusiasm was contagious. His desire to serve the nation seemed to infect everyone. I was culling resumes for positions ranging from lifelong secretaries looking to become White House secretaries to university presidents hoping to be named head of an agency or program. We had resumes from the presidents of the finest universities in the nation. I reviewed resumes from some of the most important people in the nation. Some positions we were filling were paid, some were volunteer, and everyone's resume—thousands upon thousands of them—went through my office first.

But one resume stood out above all, and it changed my life.

It was the attached cover letter that grabbed me. The gentleman looking for work was an attorney, just like my father. He had five children, just like my father. He was even the same age as my father. As I looked over his resume, I thought, "God, this could be my father," which is why I took his letter so much to heart. He stated he was desperate for work. He was unemployed and had five children, whom he dreamed of sending to college but could not afford to do so. He had worked for earlier Democratic administrations and was laid off when the Republicans took office under President Eisenhower. He had been out of steady work, jumping from job to job, ever since. Although he had a law degree, he had spent most of his career in politics; his work experience qualified him to work only in politics.

Reading the letter, I didn't picture the attorney who wrote it; I pictured my father being desperate for work, desperate to help his children attend college so they could fulfill their dreams. It didn't matter that my father was qualified to excel in a number of career fields. The similarities were enough. I thought, "What if Don and I had not been able to pay our own way into college and my father had hit hard times? Where would I be today?" I was desperate to help this man, so I put his resume on the top of the pile. I hoped that by placing his resume at the top, I could subtly convince the higher-ups to employ him.

Later that evening, I spoke to my father on the phone and told him about the attorney and his letter and how I had placed his resume on the top of the pile. I expected my father to be proud of me and commend me for having such a big heart. Instead, he admonished me, telling me that I was doing a disservice to the nation by playing favorites. My job, he reminded me, was to pass on only the best of the best. He told me to let the attorney's sad situation become a lesson to me. Politics is a tough life, he said. You're always dependent on your party staying in power and sometimes, even if it does, the new representative may replace you with one of his friends. He said people with careers in politics are always dependent on others for their work and are never in charge of their own destinies. If I stayed in politics, he said, I would never be my own man and would one day wake up and see that out-of-work attorney staring back at me in the mirror.

That night, as I lay in bed, I thought about what my father said and I realized he was right. My goal since childhood had been to never be dependent on others, yet I had allowed myself to become just that. I saw that I was not as lucky as I'd thought I was. I had to make a choice. I went to Bobby Kennedy's classmate and closest personal friend, David Hackett, to talk over my career options. I also spoke to Sarge Shriver. He said, "If you want to be in business, don't go to law school—go to a business school." He suggested I put in an application at Harvard.

A few days later, I quit the Kennedy administration. It was a tough choice. Working for Kennedy was like working for a rock star. I felt like one of the cool kids. But I knew that leaving was the best career move for me. In retrospect, I realize that my decision to leave the Kennedy world was the combination of an epiphany and an intuitive leap. It was neither carefully nor meticulously strategized. But it was a moment of clarity that Sarge Shriver and my dad had helped me to realize. It was a predicate to some of the strategic and intuitive decisions I would have to make about real estate, financial collaborators, and even my life partner.

As I searched for a new path to take, my mind wandered back to those late-night conversations with Shriver about Joe Kennedy, and I decided I wanted to take the same path to success as Joe Kennedy had. I wanted to forge a career in business and I wanted to start it at Harvard Business School.

I moved to Boston in the summer of 1962 and was scheduled to begin school that September. It would be a new life for me. I was leaving politics behind to begin a career as a businessman. But no matter how far I fled from the nation's capital, I could not escape the reach of the Kennedy family. Ted Kennedy was running for Massachusetts senator, and when the Kennedy family learned I was in Boston, they immediately contacted me to help with the campaign.

The phone call to my apartment came from Steve Smith, asking me to meet him for lunch. Smith was JFK's brother-in-law, his close friend, and political advisor. He was a tough, Brooklyn-raised Irishman, whose family made its fortune in the tugboat industry. Steve had a special way about him—that incentivized and encouraged. When he asked you to do something, it was hard to turn him down. To make a man feel as if he could walk on water, all Smith had to do was tell him, "You did a good job" and pat him on the back. So when he asked me to join Ted Kennedy's campaign, I couldn't say no, despite having promised myself that I was finished with politics. He told me that I had been the best regional coordinator the presidential campaign had and that Ted Kennedy needed a man like me … that the Kennedy family needed me. The Kennedy family needed *me*! How could I turn him down? Besides, I had not yet started school. I had the time. And I surely had the interest. This time, I would be overseeing individual counties.

I was soon back to working long days on a political campaign—12 to 15 hours a day from the campaign headquarters on Tremont

Street in Boston. The campaign was going great. We won the Democratic primary in September and were sure Kennedy would win the Senate seat. Unfortunately, when school started that month, I was still working long days on the campaign. I didn't have enough time for schoolwork and my grades were suffering.

Although I never missed a class, I had very little time to study, and it really showed. My marketing professor, Dr. Theodore Levitt, was aware of the double life I was leading—student by day and cog in the Kennedy political machine by night. He was also aware that my schoolwork was suffering because of it.

Levitt was one of the sharpest marketing minds in the history of this great nation, best known for his years spent as editor of the *Harvard Business Review* and for popularizing the term *globalization*. He took his area of expertise very seriously and was disgusted by students who treated their time at Harvard lightly, which meant that he was disgusted with me. By mid-October, his tolerance was exhausted. He believed I was wasting my time, his time, and the school's resources by masquerading as a student who cared about learning. In class one morning, as I sat bleary-eyed from a long night of working on the campaign and wishing I had had a third cup of coffee before class, Professor Levitt called on me to open the recitation of the case for that day's class. Harvard pioneered the case method of teaching, and each student was expected to read, master, and be prepared to recite the facts and technical details of the relevant case while being grilled on the theories of marketing by the professor. Nobody knew in advance who was going to be called on. So, there was an extra incentive for each student to be well prepared to avoid embarrassment.

I was probably about 8 or 10 rows up from the front of the class, trying to hide from the professor's accusing eyes, so I was startled when he called on me. I stumbled to my feet and muttered some superficial, irrelevant things, revealing that I was completely unprepared and ignorant about the case or the topic. Levitt was irritated. He threw a piece of chalk at me and stared with biting, stone-cold eyes. "Sit down, Mr. Corbett," he said sternly. "You are not prepared."

Maybe in some schools across the country today, getting called on when you're not prepared isn't a big deal, but back then it was a huge embarrassment. The rare student who was not able to recite a case was seen as a failure. And at "The B school," as it's often called, failure is not an option. It meant that you didn't have what it took to be a Harvard businessman and you didn't understand the value of the Harvard method and all it stood for in terms of professional connections and natural opportunities. Getting in to Harvard B School was one thing. Staying in and proving your worth was something else entirely.

My immersion in the Kennedy campaign probably put a chip on my shoulder and caused me to believe that I was in a bubble, able to float through the tedium of business school, protected by my association with the Kennedys, given a free pass to success, especially since I was working my butt off for the Kennedy machine. That bubble was popped by Professor Levitt, whose admonishment made me feel as if I'd been put over his knee and spanked in front of the class. I had never been so humiliated in school in my life. Everyone in Harvard Business School was a brainiac, and despite my brag-worthy standing with the Kennedy family, I realized that I was the school screw-up. And it was not cool.

After class, I tried to slip out the door without Professor Levitt seeing me. But I couldn't escape him. "Where are you going now?" he bellowed. The entire class stopped their exit to watch our engagement. "To campaign headquarters, I bet!" he continued. I nodded yes, too embarrassed to squeak words from my mouth. He motioned for me to approach his desk so that we could have a private conversation. The rest of the class filed out, leaving just the two of us in the sanctuary of the Harvard lecture hall. I kept my head bowed, still afraid to meet the gaze of my genius professor, who was obviously about to preach to me about how I was wasting my education.

"If you go down to Tremont Street right now, you have two options," he lectured. "Stay there and quit school, or quit the campaign and make school your only concern. You cannot continue with both. You cannot stay at Harvard if you stay with the campaign.

"It's now 10:30 in the morning," he continued. "I will be here until noon. Meet me here at 11:45 to tell me your decision."

I drove downtown and asked to speak to Smith privately. He brought me into his office and I told him what had happened in class. Smith offered a fatherly smile and said, "You've done a great job for us, but let's be honest. You belong at Harvard. We need you there, so that you can come back with the skills they'll give you. Go back to school and call me when you graduate. You'll always have a place here." And he meant it.

I quit the campaign that day, hunkered down at Harvard, and became one of the better students in my class. But my dream of having those Kennedy presidential connections when I graduated soon turned into a waking nightmare on November 22, 1963. I had a noon finance class that semester. I don't remember the topic, but I will never forget what I learned a little past 12:30 p.m. that day. A faculty member ran into the classroom and whispered something to my professor, whose face dropped only for a split second. Though it was obvious that he'd been given bad news, it didn't seem earth-shattering. I was wrong. "The president has been shot in Dallas," he said. He then took a deep breath and returned to his lesson plan.

"What?" I shouted to the professor. I wasn't close enough to the president to call him a friend, but I had been with him on few occasions and I had associated with quite a few of his close friends. My concern for his well-being wasn't just about his being president. He was a real person to me, flesh and bone, whose words inspired me, not just a handsome face on a television screen. I needed to know more about what happened. The professor didn't know any more; few people in the nation did at that point. I squirmed in my seat for the remainder of the class, desperate for news. I wanted to run from the room and find the nearest television or radio, but I knew that doing so would incur the wrath of my professor, who forbade leaving class early for any reason. Although I feared the worst, I was convinced that if the president had been killed, the messenger would have included that information. Maybe it was only a shoulder wound or some other minor injury. Maybe the president would be discharged from the hospital before my class even ended.

Thirty minutes after the initial news, another messenger rushed into the classroom with a dreadful update. "The president is dead," he said.

JFK is dead? I thought. It didn't seem possible. He was the nation's larger-than-life leader, the man who excited the country, the man who was going to lead the nation to greener pastures. JFK was the type of man I expected would live forever, never aging one bit. He was the once and future president, our King Arthur. JFK couldn't be murdered.

In retrospect, calling his presidency Camelot and he our King Arthur was fitting, because King Arthur's Camelot was also brought down by evildoers who hated the king simply because he represented the ultimate good. But when the news of Kennedy's murder was announced, I was not thinking in terms of literary irony. In fact, I could barely think at all. I was in total shock. What transpired next in class was even more shocking. I expected the professor to suspend class and allow us to return to our homes to mourn with the rest of the nation. Instead, he simply said, "Oh, my Lord," took a few moments to digest the news, and then returned to the lesson plan as though he'd been told about some minor fender-bender. Perhaps he didn't care for JFK so was not as upset by the news. Perhaps he was in such shock he didn't know how to react. I hope it was the latter. If it was the former, I feel sad for him. In a nation that offers such amazing opportunities and does not oppress its citizens, anyone who doesn't mourn the death of his president is cold-hearted indeed. In times of great national grief, party lines and politics must always be pushed aside.

My professor continued his lesson, but I don't think anyone in class listened to a word he said. Our minds were in Dallas, wondering what happened, as well as in Washington, DC, wondering what the fate of our nation would be.

Following class, I returned to my residence hall and, like the rest of the nation, spent the next few days glued to my television and radio, mourning the loss of one of the greatest leaders in this nation's history, trying to figure out how we would move on as a nation. The loss of JFK was a tremendous setback. Vice President Lyndon Johnson, who became president upon JFK's death, was a solid leader, but he was not JFK. He was not the new blood this nation needed. He was more of the old guard. He wasn't the type of president who could inspire the entire nation to take part in building a better country.

This was also a personal setback for me. I did not have an "in" with the Johnson regime as I did with the Kennedy family. No job would be waiting for me in Johnson's White House upon graduation. I feared my lot in life would be to return to Rochester and work for either Eastman Kodak or Xerox, the area's two major companies. I even imagined that I would have to resign myself to living an average life.

CHAPTER 10

I Was Once One of the Most-Hated Men in the Kennedy Empire

After graduation, I decided to give Steve Smith a call anyway. I figured he could at least provide me with a letter of recommendation on behalf of the Kennedy family, which was equivalent to showing up to a job interview with the key to the city. When I called, he told me to visit him at his office on Park Avenue in New York and we would discuss my future. At the meeting, we skipped formalities and small talk and jumped right into the business at hand. He one-upped the letter of recommendation I had in mind and offered me a job as his assistant in the Kennedys' New York business office.

Smith was the family's business manager as well as campaign manager, charged with overseeing their multimillion-dollar portfolio of stocks, oil, gas, and real estate. He explained that his busy schedule often took him away from the business office and he needed someone he could trust to keep him up to date on everything going on. He also said he wanted someone to delve into the office's past transactions and write up detailed reports on them for him.

The moment had a magical character to it. I was suddenly transported to another dimension and into the inner sanctum of the world of political and economic power at the heart of American business. My hard work and earlier successes for the Kennedys followed by my eventual success at Harvard established a special bond between Smith and me, based on trust and performance. I had earned my wings, but now it was time to learn how to really fly. My goodness, I was a lucky guy. But I knew that it wasn't just luck.

Of course, I didn't need more than a split second before deciding to accept the offer. Who would turn down a job in the Kennedys' business office? A few weeks later, I was living in New York and once again working for the Kennedy family. I was paid $12,500 a year. Even by 1964 standards, that was low, but it was enough to pay for an apartment in Manhattan, three meals a day, and a few beers a week. The money didn't matter to me. I was in my early twenties and working for one of the most-prestigious families in the history of this great nation.

I was back in the groove, back where I belonged and where I was wanted—but not by everybody. Ever since Joe Kennedy stepped away from the daily grind of his office, sometime in the 1950s, the office's employees had operated the business virtually unchecked. Smith had been hired to replace the old man as head of the business office, but the Kennedy campaigns and other political missions took him away from the office so often that he had little idea what was actually going on there. The employees had no one looking over their shoulders to make sure they were doing their jobs correctly, or at all, for that matter. So it shouldn't have been a surprise that I was not welcomed with open arms when I was hired in 1964 to report directly to Smith.

At some point during my first few weeks on the job, the office manager, Tom Walsh, let me know exactly how everyone felt about me. The normal routine for Friday evenings was to have drinks at Charlie Brown's, a popular happy-hour spot in the lobby of our office building, above Grand Central Station on Park Avenue. I arrived an hour or two after most of the guys in the office. I had been working late getting settled into my routines and responsibilities. Walsh was already three martinis deep and had the type of loose tongue that only a lot of alcohol and unexpressed anger can cause. I sat down next to him and tried to make small talk, explaining how happy I was to be working in the office and that I was looking forward to combing through the office files and reporting back to Smith how well everything was going. Walsh was a balding, heavyset man with gray hair and glasses, a constant sourpuss. On this night, however, he looked especially pissed off.

"You're just a pain in my ass!" he slurred, his lips spraying as he hit the P in pain.

I was taken aback and muttered a shocked, "What?"

"You heard me!" he stammered, swaying a bit in his stool. "You're just a plain upstart who wants to get me fired so you can take my job. Now get away from me!"

I tried to assure him that the last thing I wanted was his job, but his inebriation made reasoning with him impossible. I left the bar a few minutes later, went home, and stewed in anger and concern for my job. By morning, I rationalized that he didn't hate me, he was afraid of me. My job was to "tattle" on the goings-on. Before my arrival, the Kennedy family was never tipped off if an employee made a bad financial decision. The office staff looked out for each other's best interests rather than the Kennedys' fortune. Mistakes, I figured, were swept under the carpet. When the cat is away, the mice will play. I was the new cat.

Returning to work on Monday, I felt the tension everywhere I went. People said hello to me, but the greetings were cold, as if they felt they had no choice about saying hello. As I poked through file cabinets, people around me stopped whatever they were doing and coldly stared me down as if I were public enemy number one.

I saw that everyone in the office shared Walsh's opinion of me. They all thought I was a menace. I promised myself that I would not allow the desire to be liked to affect my duties. Smith had hired me to provide him with honest reports and I promised myself that was exactly what I would provide, regardless of how many enemies it made me along the way.

The situation was beyond awkward and not how I envisioned my first major career break. I drew on my years of dealing with embarrassment over my mother. I had learned to put on a mask that others could not see past. My ability to wear an emotional costume led my officemates to believe that I was not bothered by their antics in the least and that I was a hard-nosed businessman who would do my job regardless of their opinion. But underneath my costume, I was miserable. I felt alone. No one wants to be hated.

Luckily, in August 1964, just two months after my prison sentence in the Kennedy business office began, Smith sprung me. The Democratic National Convention was being held that month, and he wanted me to come along. Politics was calling again. I was excited to be leaving the negative atmosphere of the office to travel with Bobby Kennedy, one of the most exciting and beloved men in the nation, as he sized up his options for political office. I was looking forward not only to the excitement and the wild pace but also to the royal treatment that I presumed the Kennedy gang would surely receive wherever they went.

Boy was I naïve. When we arrived at the Democratic National Convention in New Jersey, instead of fanfare and a welcome, we were all treated as if we were uninvited party crashers.

The present-day primary election system was not fully in place yet nationally. Only 16 states held the kind of primary that has become commonplace since the late twentieth century. All of the remaining states held back and worked through the politics of who might be their nominee in what was then, quite literally, smoke-filled, back-rooms in which men of local and regional influence would broker for votes and possible positions in the new administration. Candidates were chosen by powerbrokers, not by the people. Today I sometimes think they're chosen as much by the press as by the parties. But in the 1950s and 1960s, the power of personalities in politics was alive and well. There were individuals who could leverage huge amounts of political power. One of them was Lyndon Baines Johnson (LBJ), Kennedy's vice president, who had ascended to the presidency only because of JFK's assassination.

LBJ had risen from the dust of Texas small-town politics and latched onto local wealth and political power through his own skills and the connections he achieved through his wife, Lady Byrd, and her prominent and wealthy family. LBJ made his own wealth and as a US senator, he had become one of the heavy-handed power-brokers in Congress. He was a brilliant political strategist who called in favors and held little-known information over the heads of his colleagues in exchange for votes and support.

And now LBJ was the incumbent, having served as president for more than two years. He had already assured his nomination at the convention by securing the promises from the majority of the dele-gate states to choose him as their state's Democratic candidate in the presidential election. Even with his incumbency and his substantial power, as the convention approached, the overcautious LBJ became concerned that Bobby's popularity could cause the Democratic del-egates to renege on their promises and nominate Bobby instead, even though he wasn't a candidate.

This was not an unfounded concern. It could have happened, as it did in the 1960 presidential election when JFK received the nomi-nation. LBJ had thought he had it wrapped up. Adding more fuel to the fire was the bad blood that existed between LBJ and Bobby.

Bobby and LBJ were longtime enemies; in fact, they detested each other. Bobby was publicly against his brother's naming LBJ his vice president. He did not think LBJ was qualified; what's more, he didn't think LBJ was trustworthy. JFK had no choice but to select LBJ because of two realities: (1) JFK, a Harvard-trained northerner with a Boston accent, needed a strong southerner to win the more conservative southern and rural votes; (2) LBJ had already forced his way into being named for the position through the control he personally exercised within the Democratic party.

Once JFK was elected and Bobby was named attorney general, the feuding between Bobby and Johnson ramped up. The Kennedys didn't help matters. JFK and Bobby would often call for meetings on national affairs and not invite LBJ, undermining him as vice president.

LBJ resented the Kennedys because of their wealth, their education, and their fancy northern ways; what's more, he had carefully planned to be the 1960 presidential candidate. Before JFK swooped into the campaign, LBJ had been the handpicked choice of the Democratic leaders. Kennedy parachuted into the presidential race out of nowhere to win the candidacy and I doubt Johnson ever recovered from the sting of that loss. I believe he hated the entire Kennedy family, convinced that he, not Kennedy, had worked hard to create the kind of political machine and base to lead the country. He believed that he, not JFK or Bobby, had worked hard enough personally in the political trenches to earn the right to be president.

JFK had been a fabulously popular president and his popularity grew mythically following the assassination. Bobby's reputation had also grown through his role as US Attorney General. He was a dynamic, young, powerful, and attractive figure. Even though LBJ loathed him, he knew that Bobby was the new, very visible face of the Kennedy family. It was conceivable that if Bobby gave a powerful speech, he could sway the delegates before the nomination of the Democratic candidate and, again, steal the nomination that LBJ thought was rightfully his.

As president, LBJ was playing the role of Wizard of Oz at the convention, pulling strings and pressing buttons behind the scenes to affect the delegations and make absolutely certain that neither Bobby nor the Kennedy machine would steal his thunder, steal his presidency again. Marvin Watson, LBJ's chief aide, was assigned to make sure that none of us in Bobby's entourage were allowed on the convention floor. And Bobby was not scheduled to speak until the final day of the convention, after LBJ had officially been nominated as the Democratic presidential candidate. To ensure that Bobby did not win over the delegates in backroom deals, the Kennedy team was even excluded from many of the major parties and events in the days leading up to the nomination. Bobby was exiled from the inside workings of the political process.

But Bobby *did* speak at the convention, as planned by LBJ. And it was fabulously choreographed. Before Bobby spoke, a short film about his brother was shown to the convention audience. Bobby then appeared on stage, greeted by a 22-minute eruption of applause. I remember how moved Bobby was by that ovation. His eyes teared. The film on his brother had been emotional and moving, and the warmth and embrace of the crowd were intensely powerful. He stood at the podium, glimmering under the lights, glowing in the adoration of the crowd, and his eyes literally glistened with a combination of electric political energy and the sadness of the circumstances— both the memory of his brother's death and Johnson's manipulation of the convention against him. It was one of the most moving public moments I've ever witnessed.

Bobby's speech lived up to the extended applause. He spoke from the heart, somberly retelling his big brother's accomplishments and what the Democratic Party and the presidency meant to his brother. He even threw his support to LBJ, which must have further irked the presidential candidate. By doing so, Bobby came off as the bigger man.

Bobby's speech told the people of the United States that while his brother may have been one of the most beloved leaders in its history, the nation was bigger than one man. He reminded us that with or without a Kennedy, it was up to the people to make the country succeed.

Bobby's address to the convention was more than a speech. It was his debut as a national political force, and it was the basis for his becoming a legend. Before his brother's murder, Bobby was the family's taskmaster, the guy who managed the politics and the elections from behind the scenes. His organizational skills were inspirational. He was also one of the most politically and factually intelligent people I've ever met. Bobby understood the details and implications of national and international issues, and he could speak on or debate any topic with only a moment's notice. And while the Kennedys were known for their competitive natures, Bobby was the most competitive of them all—far more so than JFK had been.

In a curious way, Bobby's relationship with JFK had been something like mine with my older brother, Don. For many years, Bobby felt that he played second fiddle to Jack. I believe that one of the more powerful motivating forces driving Bobby was his desire to prove his worth to his family, the nation, and to himself. He was prepared and able to put himself into overdrive to outwork, outthink, and outstrategize anybody. The combination of his energy, desire, and competence added to his esteem.

But intelligence, work ethic, organization, and competitiveness are not always enough to make for a successful political candidate. Personality is critical. Following JFK's assassination, it was assumed that Bobby would be the family's new top political dog, but it was not certain. Bobby had the mind for politics and was thought to be the brightest Kennedy son. But the family was unsure if he had the personality for elected office. He was always the backroom guy, the strategist who knew all the numbers and details. The 1964 convention proved that Bobby was far more than a back-office guru. It was unfortunate that it took the death of his big brother to showcase that side of him.

After the convention, Kennedy's circle returned to New York and regrouped. The strategizing was intense and very focused—focused on how to get to the White House. The decision was made that Bobby would resign as US attorney general and begin his elected career as a member of the New York State Senate. Though it was a state rather than a national position, it was viewed as a strategic first step toward national elected office.

The Kennedy family treated this local campaign as if it were a national one, calling in friends and family to staff the effort. This was not just a state senate race; it was the first step toward the White House. And everybody was on board. Old prep school and law school friends made up his closest team of advisors and Smith was named the campaign manager. That boded well for me because Smith trusted me, and I knew he would provide me with a good campaign job.

Smith named me campaign coordinator for the northern region of upstate New York. The job carried with it responsibilities very different from those I had as Midwest coordinator for JFK's campaign. I was not a shopkeeper making sure each district had its campaign materials. I was coordinating Bobby's visits to each city and making sure each district had local and well-known political leaders stumping for him throughout the election. When Bobby visited a city, I personally coordinated his events and speaking engagements and did the same for the local leaders when they were planning rallies in support of Bobby in their respective cities.

I was one of the few people to obtain a senior position in the campaign who wasn't a family member or an old school friend. I felt lucky—and intimidated. I knew I would always be something of an outsider, especially when I watched Bobby and his old friends clowning around as if they were at a fraternity party rather than an election meeting. I fantasized about truly being a part of their inner circle. But I was fabulously lucky just to be a part of the inner workings of the campaign and to be in a position to watch and participate in the often-bombastic dynamics of the Kennedy family.

But I wasn't always treated as an outsider. Curiously, Bobby and his closest friends and family treated me like a younger brother at times, dispensing advice to me and tousling my hair in a ball-busting manner whenever I had a great idea for the campaign. I participated in the fun, and I was allowed to be close to the inside. Nevertheless, it was always a very tightly run campaign shop, and I was expected to function professionally and efficiently.

The family name and his reputation were too well known and too powerful a political force. He easily won the Democratic primary and then steamrolled Keating, defeating him by over 700,000 votes in the general election.

After the election, I returned to the Kennedys' New York business office and picked up where I left off—as public enemy number one, working for Smith. If the office employees hated me before the election, I figured they most certainly would despise me even more following it. They were stuck in a monotonous nine-to-five hell while I rubbed shoulders with Bobby and his pals. I figured that they would be wildly jealous.

Reducing my appeal even more, rather than putting me back to work analyzing the Kennedys' business portfolio, Smith named me the coordinator of the traveling John F. Kennedy Presidential Library exhibit. From 1964 through the end of 1965, an exhibit memorializing JFK traveled the country. It displayed his presidential desk and numerous other items, including photographs and documents from his presidential years. My job was to contact authorities in each city it visited and make sure everything was set for its arrival, such as a proper welcoming party and publicity. I was also tasked with ensuring that the locations were secured, that all the proper permits were obtained, and all expenditures associated with the traveling exhibit were in order.

In late 1965, I was pulled off the exhibit and told to return to my full-time duties in the business office, which I found comical. Return? I had never really started. But I was a recognized rising star in the Kennedy Empire and I was determined to use the business office to further impress the family hierarchy. I spent dozens of hours digging into the complexities of the Kennedy business portfolio and analyzed everything I could find about their holdings, cash flow, assets, liabilities, and returns. Within weeks of my return to the office, I had identified what I believed to be an opportunity in real estate for the Kennedy portfolio.

After long, careful analysis, I determined that the 15-story Banker's Trust building they owned on 14th Street in downtown New York should be sold. The building had renters locked into long-term leases specifying that their rents could be increased only by a certain percentage in the future, over a set number of years. I saw that within a few years, the costs of maintenance, upkeep, and property taxes alone would not be covered by the rent unless the renters agreed to a substantially larger rent increase or were bought out of their leases so that the Kennedys could sign on new, higher-paying tenants.

I put a few feelers out in the real estate world, and a local broker named Lew Sarasy called me at the office within a week with the name of a potential buyer, a buyer willing to take it off our hands at a *very* generous price. I was not sure why he thought he could make a profit off the building when the Kennedys could not. Perhaps he had not analyzed the building's finances as thoroughly as I had.

I was bursting with excitement! I was about to make my first big real estate transaction and earn a profit for the Kennedy family. I was going to be a hero! I ran down the hall to Tom Walsh's office, burst through the door, told him about the interested buyer, and said I thought we should take the deal.

Walsh—sober this time—looked me straight in the eyes and spat out, "Fuck you! Get the fuck out of my office!" It took every ounce of restraint I had not to leap across his desk and show off my boxing skills. I could not understand what was going on with this man. We were there to make the Kennedy family money! Why didn't he want to do his job?

I was determined to get an answer. That night, I stormed over to Charlie Brown's after work, ready to confront Walsh. By the time I arrived, he was at least *four* martinis deep, though, fortunately, not yet venomously drunk. He was in a happy-go-lucky state, even happy to see me.

He waved to me from across the bar. "Take a seat!" he said. I was a bit hesitant, unsure what to make of his sudden change of heart, but I knew from experience (including with my mother) that anyone in that sort of drunken state would tell the truth. Drunks historically have a hard time lying. I didn't have to dig for the answer. As soon as I sat down next to him, he spilled out his soul to me, explaining that no one at the office wanted to buy or sell property, a caution that could be traced back to Joe Kennedy's time in the office, because anyone who made the slightest mistake was fired. Losing a dime in the cushion of a sofa was looked down on by the Kennedy patriarch. "If I tell you to paint those windows black, then *do it!*" Joe would yell at his employees. The old man had instilled so much fear in the people working at the office that they stopped looking for deals and only managed the properties and stocks already in the portfolio. They acted on a deal only when ordered to do so by someone in the family, because only a Kennedy could make a mistake and not get fired.

Walsh said there was a time when everyone in the office had the go-getter attitude I possessed and all dreamt of making the Kennedys a lot of money, but their spirits had been crushed. Though Joe Kennedy had retired, the Kennedy family still lived by the same business code. They would fire anyone who made a mistake. Brilliant market analysts were reduced to property and stock managers. Their only job was to not lose their jobs.

I was rocking the boat, he explained. I was the first new blood brought into the office in a long time and everyone was afraid of the threat I represented. They didn't hate me because I was a tattle-tale. They hated me because they thought I was going to get overly aggressive and cost people their jobs. Compounding their negative view of me was that no one in the office respected my business savvy. They thought I was a politician, not a businessman. They were not impressed with my Harvard MBA. My only real world experience was in politics.

I pointed out that Smith trusted me enough to hire me to evaluate the business deals, and Smith was his boss, after all. Walsh just laughed, saying that Smith was a good political tactician, but his business knowledge was limited. He was in over his head when it came to understanding the Kennedys' business portfolio. Smith's job was basically just a thank-you for his dedication to the family; he was not expected to do any work. He just collected paychecks to tide him over until the next election rolled around. Walsh made it clear that Smith had hired me to explain the business deals to him simply so it would appear as if he knew what was going on at the office. In reality, the only person who could approve any new deal was Walsh, and he said he was not going to approve of anything that was not a Kennedy's idea, because only a Kennedy could lose money and not get into trouble. He said if I went over his head, Smith would be too afraid to go ahead with any deal. Like the rest of the office, he would not want to be known as the man who lost the Kennedys money.

The Banker's Trust building was not a huge deal. If it lost money the Kennedys might not have ever noticed. But it's a slippery slope, explained Walsh. If he allowed me to make that deal, he was afraid I'd become emboldened and look for bigger and far riskier deals that could get everyone into trouble.

I was crushed by these revelations. My dream job suddenly became a dead-end one. I had expected to use the Kennedy office as my springboard to the future. But I saw now that I was sidelined.

I pouted for at least a few weeks, though I went to work every day and continued to perform my duties. I researched and wrote detailed reports in layman's terms on the Kennedys' investments but ceased looking for new ways to earn the family money. I became like everyone else in the office—a man with no dream, a man who desired only to keep his job.

11

Mentored by an Invalid

One day, while filing some papers in a storage closest, I stumbled on a treasure trove of information—a filing cabinet that contained old tax returns, income and expense statements, business plans, and market analyses of business deals spearheaded by Joe Kennedy himself while he was in his business prime. It was an inside look at one of the more street-smart businessmen in our nation. At that time, Joe Kennedy had suffered a debilitating stroke and could no longer communicate. Occasionally, a nurse would wheel him into the office and staff members would greet him politely. We could see that he was mentally alert, but his body trembled as he tried to make hand motions and speak. He was completely helpless and only grew more frustrated with the effort.

Yet, I saw that I could learn all of this brilliant businessman's secrets by combing through those files. Harvard Business School had nothing on the education I got from studying Joe Kennedy's work. I immersed myself in the project and learned seven important lessons from those files:

1. Owning a major real estate gem, like the Merchandise Mart, is like having an oil well. It produces a steady stream of tax-efficient income.

2. While diversification of investments is considered a conventional business strategy, a single, distinctive, revenue producing asset, such as the Mart, can protect a huge investment portfolio. But those are rare and exceptional golden geese.

3. Intimately understand your market so that you will know the best time to buy and sell real estate. People who lose money

in real estate do so because they buy it when the price is too high, hold on to it too long, or sell it too quickly.

4. Take educated risks; never jump into any business deal blindly. Every business deal is a risk. Nothing is a sure thing. But if you carefully analyze everything, you can determine which projects are worth the risk and which are not. However, experience and wisdom over the years feeds effective intuition.

5. Don't be afraid to think outside the box. Earning a profit on any deal always comes down to imagination.

6. Remember the cardinal rule of business schools: use someone else's money if you can. By doing so, if the investment sinks, your personal finances will not.

7. While careful study and meticulous analysis are important, intuition—gut sensibilities—play an important role in business decisions. And those are not things learned in books. Otherwise anybody could become a Joe Kennedy—or, in current (2019) terms, a Donald Trump.

Although these were all lessons taught in business school, it was only through Kennedy's files that I was able to clearly understand how he actually applied them in his business dealings. I was able to study his every success along with his failures, what worked and what did not.

Perhaps the best example of what made Joe Kennedy a business genius was his greatest financial success—the Merchandise Mart in Chicago. The Merchandise Mart opened in 1930 on the banks of the Chicago River in downtown Chicago. It was the largest building in the world, containing four million square feet of commercial space. It was so large it had its own postal code. The Mart was built by Marshall Field & Company, a once powerful department-store conglomerate.

The company built the Mart for its wholesale business needs so that it could consolidate furniture warehousing into one location. Field then leased out space to other furniture wholesalers, creating a unique and singular destination for all furniture wholesale goods. Never before had any company undertaken such a venture. It was a standout as a business and unique architecturally.

The art-deco design of the building was distinctive and more than 80 years later, it remains astounding. It comprises an 18-story warehouse, a department store, and a 25-story skyscraper. The interior features marble piers, bronze trim, long corridors with terrazzo floors, and six and one-half miles of display windows. But it wasn't long after this shopping castle was built and occupied that Marshall Field discovered that it was a huge financial burden.

In 1931, a year after it opened, the Mart lost Marshall Field $5 million—a lot of money back then. The following year it lost another $8 million. The development rebounded during World War II, when Field rented space to hundreds of government offices. Then, the dedication of the Pentagon in 1943 unseated the Mart's status as the world's largest building and lured away many of its government rental contracts.

Marshall Field was desperate to sell to fund their expansion into suburban malls and to make a claim for a refund of World War II excess profits tax, but no local buyer was interested, even though it was shopped around endlessly.

That's when Joe Kennedy swooped in.

Although many US millionaires had suffered economic losses during the Great Depression, Joe Kennedy had thrived. He invested in alcohol, real estate, Hollywood, oil, and more. When one of these investments would falter, he would sink more money into another and turn a profit to make up for the loss. A vital lesson: diversification.

Kennedy then used his profits to buy real estate from those in financial disarray, acquiring additions to his portfolio at well-below-market prices. He knew which developers and property owners were desperate to get out of debt and that Marshall Field was one of them. Kennedy was in a position to "help out" by purchasing the financially burdensome Mart. The old man had watched carefully and waited, and he knew he had Field by the balls.

In 1946, Kennedy made a $12 million offer for what 15 years earlier had been a $30 million investment. He offered to pay $18 million less—60%—than the Mart had cost to be built. What's more, his terms of sale were nearly draconian. He would pay only $1 million up front, paying off the rest in monthly installments over two years.

Marshall Field countered with $13 million and was terrified that Kennedy would walk away from the deal. But, he agreed without so much as blinking.

Another lesson to be learned from Joe Kennedy: know your market as well as the people in it making decisions.

Kennedy transformed the building and its use. It remained dedicated to wholesale warehousing and office space, but he opened it up to the general public. Today, it's common for individuals to shop at wholesale stores and outlets such as IKEA and Costco, but it was a very new idea at the time. Kennedy popularized the notion of individuals buying goods at wholesale prices. He knew that the public was ready to embrace the wholesale shopping concept. Another lesson: take educated risks.

But the old man wasn't done yet. To further increase the volume of people coming to visit the Mart, he turned it into a tourist destination as well as a shopping destination. The Marshall Field people had had the same idea, but they didn't have the know-how to make it work. They offered guided tours of the Mart, but there were no other attractions for people to see. Kennedy filled that gap by creating the Mart's Merchants' Hall of Fame, which immortalized "outstanding American merchants." Eight merchants were inducted, each with a bronze bust—four times larger than life size—rising up from pillars on the river side of the plaza. These massive bronze statues remain a popular tourist destination in Chicago. A lesson in creativity: think outside the box.

Kennedy's plan worked, enabling him to increase the rent on the tenants already in place. He signed new tenants who wanted their wholesale stores to benefit from the increase in foot traffic. Finally, he was able to make his monthly payments on the purchase without actually using his own savings. He would collect the rent from all his tenants, pay himself a large salary with the monthly earnings, pay employees, and have enough left over to make the monthly installment. Except for his initial $800,000 investment, Kennedy was able to purchase the Merchandise Mart without ever having to dip into his own capital. His final lesson: never use your own money.

The Merchandise Mart was the single most reliable of all the Kennedy family investments. In 1998, the family sold it for $650 million.

The more I learned about Joe Kennedy the more I realized that the business world was my true calling in life and I dedicated as much time as possible to studying the old man's business practices. Between 1966 and 1968, I worked in the Kennedy office nine to five and then stayed in the office late into the evening, often till after midnight, combing through Joe's files. I did this for two years, during which time I grew even closer to Smith.

Because Smith was impressed by my business and political smarts, when Robert Kennedy decided to run for president of the United States in 1968, Smith named me treasurer for the entire campaign. This was my big break. I was a rock star again, working for a Kennedy presidential campaign and a future president, only this time in a high-level, highly visible, and highly valued position.

I soon learned that having a high-level position also meant I had to deal with high levels of stress. My job included preparing and managing campaign budgets for each state primary—determining how much we could spend on campaign materials, hotels, airlines, food, and so on—and ensuring that we stuck to them.

Shortly after Bobby announced his intention to run, LBJ announced: "If nominated, I will not run; if elected, I will not serve." He exited the election process entirely. His elected term had been a very a difficult one, dealing with the Vietnam War, civil rights, and huge antigovernment protests. I don't think he had the desire to continue on as president—or the energy to fight Bobby for the Democratic candidacy.

But Bobby was not the frontrunner. The Democratic establishment was backing Vice President Hubert Humphrey. The nonprimary states had pledged their convention delegate votes to Humphrey. If Bobby was going to become the Democratic candidate, he would have to win the primaries, essentially forcing the delegates from the nonprimary states to support him. They would not want to risk a coup within the Democratic Party by going against popular opinion.

Bobby's toughest competition in the Democratic primaries was Eugene McCarthy, a US senator from Minnesota, who was campaigning on a very strong antiwar platform. Some believed he was running only to stop Bobby from winning. If McCarthy won the national Democratic primary, it was believed he would kowtow to Humphrey and accept a spot as his vice president rather than trying to force the delegates to change their votes.

The primary season did not start off well for Bobby. He received only 1% of the vote in New Hampshire, 6% in Wisconsin, and 11% in Pennsylvania, losing handily to McCarthy in all three states. Then, in a crushing embarrassment, he lost to McCarthy in Massachusetts, the Kennedys' home state. It looked as if Kennedy was going to lose all of the primary bids and any shot at the nomination. As the losses mounted, so did the pressure to find a way to win. And as the pressure increased, the Kennedy money machine forced spending to increase. If the Kennedy name and Bobby's own charisma could not win primaries, then money would have to be massively infused into the contests.

In each state we stumped in, we blew the budget, spending far more than had been allocated. Despite Bobby's reputation for tight organizational control and hard-core management, the campaign was a financial disaster. It was one of the most financially irresponsible organizations I've ever encountered—other than the fiscal insanity of today's federal and state governments. Although I tried to be as rational and incisive with the campaign budget as possible, I was frequently overruled and spending often deteriorated into uncontrolled madness. The higher-ups acted as if money was no object, and in fact it wasn't. Since our fundraising efforts were mediocre, we were forced to draw on the personal trust accounts of the Kennedy family, which was approximately $5 million ($20 million in today's dollars) to get back into the White House.

But I was hired to do a job, and even though Bobby seemed fine with the spending, it was my duty to say something about the variances between the budgets and actual expenditures. How do you tell the Kennedys they're being financially irresponsible? How would they react to being reprimanded by someone whom they considered a kid? Afraid to act, I kept silent on the matter as long as I could.

A few days before the Indiana primary, while going over the budget numbers in our Indiana campaign headquarters, I finally had to speak up. Cash flow was getting completely out of hand. We had budgeted $3 million for the entire Indiana primary campaign and had already spent substantially more than that. I told Smith we had already racked up a $1 million bill with Eastern Airlines and we were less than two months into the primary election. We were also wildly overspending on hotels and food, flying campaign people all over the country, putting them up in five-star hotels, and providing them with gourmet meals.

The spending seemed ridiculous to me, and I told Smith we had to begin making some cuts. Before he could answer me, however, Bobby shut me up with what amounted to a dressing-down in his strong, clear Boston accent: "Who are you, Richard, to place a value on the presidency?" he asked in a stern, lecturing tone. "I'm running for president of the United States, and I will spend whatever it takes to win."

I saw firsthand why Tom Walsh was so afraid to screw up in the Kennedy business office. Bobby's response reminded me of what Walsh had said about Joe Kennedy's "do-as-I-say-with-no-questions-asked" attitude. I don't think I'd ever felt smaller in my life. There was nothing I could say. I was a young, baby-faced kid just a few years out of college. He was Bobby Kennedy. The argument was over.

The tension lifted somewhat on May 7, when Kennedy won the Indiana primary, earning 42% of the vote. We skipped the Ohio primary, as did all the candidates, conceding it to Stephen Young, the state's senator. Kennedy won the Nebraska primary but lost in Oregon, again to McCarthy. The primaries had become a dogfight. If Kennedy was going to win the Democratic Party nomination, he had to win California.

Which brings us full circle back to that Los Angeles hotel room.

When Kennedy realized that he was going to win the California primary, he immediately called Humphrey to playfully rub it in. Kennedy knew that winning California would propel him to victory in the remaining primary states and force the delegates from nonprimary states to support his candidacy. "Hubert, we just won California," he said gleefully over the phone. "And we're going to chase your butt all over North Dakota and the Midwest. I have this nomination!"

Humphrey took the teasing well. He was rarely antagonistic, and Kennedy respected him. Still, Humphrey must have jabbed back in jest, because Kennedy laughed at the response before wishing him well and ending the call. It was time for us to head downstairs to the ballroom, where three bullets were about to end Kennedy's life and transform my own.

After the funeral at St. Patrick's Cathedral, the funeral train ride from New York to Washington, DC, was a slow, slow ride, stopping in cities along the way so that everyone could pay their respects to Kennedy. It was completely different from the loud, cheering, explosive arrivals we had experienced for months on the campaign trail. The funeral train crowds were somber and quiet, teary-eyed, respectful, and somewhat stunned.

I did a lot of thinking on that death-train ride. I didn't have a whole lot to return to in New York. I had a dead-end job in an office where I was hated and the dubious distinction of having to settle millions of dollars in campaign bills and finalize the expenditure book for a murdered candidate. An interesting challenge perhaps, but any potential bloom on the Kennedy rose had now fatally faded.

A few days after Kennedy was buried, I looked into the mirror and saw staring back at me that poor, out-of-work, aging attorney who had written that cover letter to the JFK administration, begging for employment. For years, I thought that I would break free to become my own man, but the power and prestige that comes with being part of the Kennedy family's inner circle was hard to resist. It had pulled me back to them again and again, and I had become dependent. I needed regular doses of the Kennedy "fix" to define myself. I may not have been an alcoholic, but I had come to depend, nearly obsessively, on the Kennedy association—an addiction no less powerful than my mother's.

I love the Kennedys with all my heart. They gave me my big break in life. I owe them more than I could ever repay. I probably could have worked for them for the rest of my life and lived comfortably, but I didn't want to become another cog in the Kennedy machine. I wanted—no, I needed—more than a comfortable life. I needed to break free. I didn't want to work for anybody. I wanted to be their business equal. For that to happen, I had to take my few marbles out of the Kennedy game and assume greater control and independent responsibility for my own life.

12

It Takes Guts to Write Checks for Money You Don't Have

As I continued to assess my life and my future after Robert Kennedy's assassination, I realized that my personal finances were also a mess. I was in debt—I still owed Harvard quite a bit of money— and I could barely cover my own living expenses. And I had only myself to blame. The allure of working for the Kennedy family had blurred my vision of reality for so long that I was now near financial ruin. I was content with my low salary as long as I could brag that I worked with the Kennedys. Yet I finally had to admit that it would never be enough to sustain me.

That's when I received the call that changed my life—my friend Larry Lavan had a "can't-miss" stock deal for me.

Lavan was a young and persuasive man who used his charm and personal connections to become a business wheeler-dealer, beginning in his early twenties. His father was Peter Lavan, a partner in one of New York's largest law firms, Stroock, Stroock and Lavan. One of the firm's attorneys was William vanden Heuvel, who had been the assistant to Bobby Kennedy in the US Attorney General's Office. When Bobby ran for president, vanden Heuvel joined the law firm, which then helped to garner major support for the campaign. I met Lavan through my work for the campaign and immediately realized his potential as a political and personal ally. I knew if I stayed close to him, good things would happen.

The stock deal with which he wanted my assistance revolved around an up-and-coming health-care company, Americare, run by a St. Louis native named Richard Laughlin. The stock was valued at less than $1 a share. But Lavan had been tipped off by Laughlin that the company was on the verge of making a few major announcements that would push the stock's worth to $10–$15 a share. Yes, it was what we would today call insider trading. Back then, we just called it doing business.

Lavan said if I could buy a significant number of shares, he could find me a buyer after the stock price went up. I knew Lavan was a man of his word, and I wanted in on the deal. There was just one small problem. I had only $800 in the bank and a mountain of debt. I had to find a way to get the money. I couldn't continue to sit back, play it safe, and collect my small Kennedy business office paycheck. I had to make a move. I knew that I had to take a risk sooner or later if I were ever going to amount to more than an office lackey.

I was still reeling from the death of Bobby, and it was getting to a point where I didn't care about consequences anymore. Only a man in that frame of mind could do what I did next. I wrote a check for $20,000 out of my personal checking account, which had only $800 in it. I was hoping to purchase the stock, sell the shares, and deposit the money into my account before the bank noticed the bounced $20,000 check.

It was an insane and foolhardy plan.

The day after I handed Lavan the check, my Irving Trust banker, George Kent, called me, demanding to know what the hell I was thinking. I spoke in circles for a few moments as I desperately tried to figure a way out. Kent was not in the mood for my ramblings. He told me very matter-of-factly that I was going to meet with him for lunch that day. Perfect, I thought. I'd be able to explain.

At our meeting, I insisted that it was a can't-miss deal because I had insider information. Rather than allowing him to scold me for bouncing the check, I turned the tables on him and asked him for a loan. I swore I'd be able to pay his bank back. Insanely ballsy as it was, it worked. Kent told me he would sweep my bounced check under the rug and give me a $20,000 loan to buy the stock. I know full well it wasn't my persuasive charm that won him over. If any other 30-year-old with $800 to his name—not to mention one who'd bounced a $20,000 check—had asked for a loan based on insider information, he'd have been laughed out of the bank. I had an ace in the hole. Irving Trust was one of the Kennedy family's banks. And Kent was willing to do me a favor simply because he knew my history and relationship with the Kennedys. By doing me a favor, he hoped

I would brag about the bank's kindness to the Kennedy family. Even though Irving Trust already had the Kennedys' business, a good bank knows it has to continually work to keep its top clients happy.

As I walked out of the bank that day, I wanted to run through the streets exclaiming that I'd pulled off a great hustle. Rather than bragging about my success, I continued my hustle. The next day, Lavan took me to Chase Manhattan Bank to meet with his banker, Mike Friedman. Chase Manhattan was the bank that Stroock, Stroock and Lavan used. I asked for a $40,000 loan and put my stock up as collateral. The stock was worth only $20,000, but Lavan vouched it would be worth $300,000 within a few days. Friedman agreed to the loan. Again, it was all about personal connections. Friedman could not afford to accuse Lavan, the son of one of the bank's best clients, of being a liar. Refusing the loan would have meant that he didn't believe Lavan's stock quote. Also, Friedman hoped that by helping me out he too would endear his bank to the Kennedy family and add another high-powered client to his portfolio.

A few days later, the stock climbed to $15 a share, and Lavan and I headed to Los Angeles to meet his stock buyer. After all the bullshit I had just pulled off in New York, I thought I was the slickest man in the country. But Los Angeles, a place I hadn't visited since we packed Bobby into his coffin wearing my clothes, quickly brought me back to earth.

Lavan's interested buyer offered me $750,000 for my 60,000 shares of stock. I could not believe what was happening. A week ago I was worth $800. Suddenly, I was worth $750,000! The buyer promised me he would deposit the money into my account in a few days. I said no. I got greedy. I didn't want my money in a few days. I wanted it right then and there. I was afraid he would get cold feet and back out of the deal. This was too much money for me to lose over buyer's remorse. Offended, the buyer told me the deal was off. I tried to salvage the deal by lowering the price, but it was no use. I had overplayed my hand.

Later that day I returned to New York, where I had no real career, $800 in cash, and a mountain of debt that was about to grow larger once the first loan payments were due. I was lost.

That's when broker Lew Sarasy came to the rescue.

I had remained close with Sarasy ever since Tom Walsh, the Kennedys' business office manager, nixed the Banker's Trust office building sales deal in 1965. Sarasy thought I was an up-and-comer, so he would often call me to have a few drinks and tell me about deals he had cooking. In return, I'd share fascinating stories about the campaign and the amazing things I was learning about Joe Kennedy. From time to time, Sarasy would offer me an opportunity to get in on a real estate deal with him, but I always turned him down. I would analyze the deal but always concluded that my financial portfolio was just not strong enough to get the type of loan I needed to invest.

Shortly after I returned from Los Angeles, Sarasy offered me yet another opportunity. I asked why he continued to offer me deals when I always turned him down and he said he believed in me and wanted to see me succeed. He hoped that one day I'd finally say yes and realize my potential. I had always wanted Joe Kennedy as a mentor. Little did I know that what I really needed was Lew Sarasy.

Sarasy had a client looking to sell three brownstones in New York—two on Hudson Street and one on Morton Street. The owner was moving and wanted to sell rather than be an absentee landlord. The owner did not want to sell the three brownstones to three different buyers though. They had to be bought as a group for the price of $40,000 apiece, $120,000 total.

I pulled up every piece of paperwork the city had on those properties, researching the building-inspection reports, property tax history, credit background on the renters, and so on. When my analysis was complete, I concluded that this was a *very* sound investment. Every unit was occupied, the tenants were never late with their rent, and they all had long-term leases, with rent increasing each year. The buildings did not require a great deal of renovation, and the property taxes were manageable. Rent would cover the building expenses and earn me a monthly profit for years to come. The owner was definitely not selling because the brownstones were money pits. He really did want to sell only because he was moving. This had to be an easy deal for Sarasy to find a buyer, yet he brought it to me first. I had to find a way to make it work.

I asked Sarasy if I could purchase the property with little down and pay off the rest through monthly installments. If I could work the deal just right, I could pay the installments with the income I earned from the renters, just like Joseph Kennedy had with the Mart. The property owner agreed to the deal. Why? As often happened throughout my early business career, it was because he wanted to do business with someone associated with the Kennedys. He hoped that doing so could get him in with the Kennedy family or, at the very least, allow him to brag to his friends that he did business with a Kennedy associate. We agreed that I would pay the seller $20,000 cash and he would take the rest in monthly installments over several years.

Using the stock as collateral, I took out a loan at Marine Midland, another Kennedy family bank. It was large enough to pay the down payment and renovation costs plus give me money left over to cover the first few months of payments I owed the other two banks on the stock loans. My portfolio then included three brownstones worth $120,000 and $750,000 in stock. Within a month, I went from being worth $800 to almost $1 million.

Sarasy wasn't done making me rich. The three brownstones meant I had solid collateral. Any bank in the city would give me a loan if I put the brownstones up. He told me about another brownstone up for sale at 158 West 11th Street, saying it was such a good deal that five other people were bidding on it. I had an ace in the hole, he told me. He personally knew the owner, an old lady who held several properties. He took me to her 110th Street apartment and introduced us. She asked me about my upbringing, how I got involved with the Kennedys and where I wanted my career path to take me. It was nice. It was like talking to someone's grandmother.

She loved me. Emotional costume always at the ready, I portrayed myself as a humble, small-town boy trying to make it in the big city. In truth, I was a young hustler taking advantage of the system to try to make myself rich, but she would never have guessed that. When our meeting ended, she told me she would sell me the property and agreed to the same arrangement I had made for the purchase of the other brownstones. I once again got a loan that covered the down payment and renovation costs, as well as loan payments on the other brownstones.

I was amassing more and more debt and covering it with a spider web of loans from different banks, but I wasn't concerned. I'd done my due diligence on all the properties and knew they would one day soon sell for a profit, allowing me to wipe out my debt.

Impressed by my business savvy, Sarasy offered me one final deal. He was moving to San Francisco and looking for someone to take over his real estate operation. He said he had long thought I had the chops for his business, but he had to see me in action before he could be sure. After what I pulled off that month, he was sure I could handle it. I said yes and he soon handed over to me a Rolodex filled with contacts throughout the city as well as boxes of files analyzing a multitude of buildings. He said whenever a good deal popped up, his contacts would let me know.

His contacts lived up to his word and over the next few months I purchased another few properties using the same scheme—get a loan to cover the down payment, renovations, and other loan payments. I was suddenly a man on the rise and Sarasy wasn't the only person who recognized it. Throughout this period—1968 and 1969—as I established myself as a player in real estate while holding down my Kennedy office job, I was also regularly traveling to Florida with Steve Smith to help the Kennedy family close a land deal in Fort Myers that included the Rockefeller and the Ford families. Each family purchased large plots of land congruent to one another that were then amassed into one giant area for the development of 50,000 housing units. The deal had been brought to the attention of the Kennedy family, not the business office, which is how it managed to get approved.

The gentleman who brokered the deal was Robert Troutman, Jr. Troutman had been roommates in Harvard with Joseph P. Kennedy, Jr., JFK's older brother, and he was best known for developing a voluntary approach to opening industrial jobs for African Americans. As a member of JFK's Committee on Equal Opportunity, he developed the Plans for Progress, a program to induce many of the nation's largest corporations to hire and promote African Americans. It was an early form of affirmative action except that, rather than forcing companies to hire minorities, employers were provided incentives to do so, such as tax breaks.

Like me, after the two Kennedy assassinations, Troutman left politics behind and delved into real estate and development. He was doing a masterful job at finding land in Florida, attracting investors, and selling them on the land's potential. He was a Pied Piper; people wanted to follow him. Born and raised in Atlanta, Georgia, he could relate to the people of the South. Yet he was schooled in Boston and was close to the Kennedy family, so he could relate to the Northerners, as well. There was no one Troutman couldn't sell on a deal. While he was selling the Kennedys and the other families on the Fort Myers development, he introduced me to Floyd Luckey, who, in turn, did a tremendous job of selling me on another deal.

Luckey was president of the influential Graham Family, a substantial dairy and real estate group in South Florida. A member of their family, Bob Graham, was governor of Florida at the time. The Grahams wanted to sell a large plot of land called Black Island in Lee County, near Luckey's home in Fort Myers. The land was an undeveloped island next to Bonita Springs. Luckey claimed that, if developed properly, it could be worth $20 million. That's all I needed to pique my interest.

The meeting was informal, to say the least. We used a Fort Myers beach as our boardroom and sticks and sand as our office supplies. Luckey drew a crude map of the island in the sand and split it into three sections, saying he would buy one section, I would buy another, and we'd find a third investor to purchase the last. Luckey had the equipment and the manpower to develop land. He wanted to dredge a few miles of canals into the island, clear the mangroves, and develop residential and tourist villages throughout. We could either manage the island ourselves or sell it for a substantial profit. At the end of the meeting, we shook hands. I was in. On returning to New York, I took out a $750,000 loan against the nearly half-dozen properties I owned and a short time later the Rockefellers became our third partner in the Black Island deal. In what seemed like no time at all, I already owned stock, real estate, and an island, which altogether were worth millions of dollars.

Life was good.

And it was about to get even better.

CHAPTER 13

Life Partnering

On February 26, 1970, my 32nd birthday, I received the best birthday present ever—the woman I loved agreed to marry me.

Just three months later, we said our I do's.

We'd met in September 1968, after Bobby Kennedy's assassination, when I was working long hours at the Kennedy office. A friend, Jonathan Smith, invited me over to his apartment for a cocktail party. I turned him down, but he called me around eight o'clock that evening and said to get the hell out of the office and come to the party. There was a musician playing a violin in his living room, great wine, and prep school classmates. Cornie was one of them. She had just come in from Aspen, where she was working as a skiing instructor. When we met, it was like electricity. She was down to earth, not hoity-toity, and when I heard her say, "Oh, shit!" I thought to myself, "My God, here is a real person."

When everyone else left the party, we went to a burger place on Madison Avenue. That's where I learned that we loved the same things—hunting, skiing, and photography. Later that Fall, we bought rose-colored glasses and walked up and down Madison Avenue. She was wide-open, happy, and fun to be with. Yet, she was clear about having to go back to Aspen later in the fall, and I couldn't believe she was going to leave. It felt like a divorce. She returned in the summer of 1969 and we've been together ever since.

By 1970 I was a millionaire due to owning numerous brownstones, but I was only a paper millionaire. My investments on bank statements are what declared me rich. But I did not have enough in the bank to keep me afloat if my investments failed. That reality slapped me in the face during my honeymoon.

For our honeymoon, Cornie and I visited Hawaii, Hong Kong, Thailand, Nepal, Bali, and Bangkok. It wasn't until we'd been away three months that I finally checked in with Lew Sarasy, whom I'd asked to keep an eye on my investments while I was gone.

The news was not good.

"Everything is going down the tubes!" he said. "Where the hell have you been? We've been looking for you. Things began falling apart over a month ago! Get home right now. *You're almost broke!*"

Clearly, the honeymoon was over.

I returned from the trip to find I was in financial disarray. My entire portfolio was in trouble. For a while, my real estate scheme had been working. I would take out a loan that enabled me to make the down payment on a new property and pay for renovations while leaving me enough money to cover loan payments on my other properties. I would then sell one of the properties and use some of the profit to pay back an entire outstanding loan.

However, while I was off wandering the mountains of Nepal, the economy back home had taken a downturn. Recession reared its ugly head, and people stopped buying, which is why when I called Sarasy from Bangkok, he told me I would soon be bankrupt if I didn't get back to New York to handle the situation. Some potential purchases of my properties had fallen through and my other properties for sale were garnering zero interest. With no one able to buy any of my properties, I had no way to pay back any loans in full. If I did not find a way to remedy the situation, I was going to fall too far into debt to ever climb out.

A developer in my financial situation has two options:

1. Sell cheap and cut your losses. There are always people ready to follow the Joe Kennedy motto and swoop in and take advantage of a developer in financial trouble by buying properties well below market value. Sometimes it's worth taking whatever you can get just to get out of debt.
2. Hold on to the property, continue to make the loan payments by taking out additional loans, fall further into debt, hope the market turns around before you're bankrupt, and then sell for a profit.

Luckily, I was able to exercise option two. I met with my banks and convinced them to allow me to refinance my loans, which enabled me to cover my monthly expenses through the rent I was earning and through my paltry Kennedy family monthly check. But I was barely breaking even every month, which meant that Cornie had to use her savings to help pay our household bills—rent, food, utilities, and so on. Ironically, because of my real estate portfolio, I could have walked into any bank in America, put up the deed to my property, and received a loan, but in the meantime, I was cash poor, and had to budget carefully. On paper, my property values made me a millionaire; in reality, I was flat broke. Without Cornie taking care of us, I don't know how we would have survived.

Cornie wanted to play a role in working the properties. She came to work for my real estate company and we became life and business partners. Cornie was in the trenches with our subcontractors, substantially contributing to the operation and the success of the property business. Her design talents and managerial skills have always been exceptional. The carpenters, plumbers, and electricians adored her.

After a few months, though, we realized that if we were ever going to start a family, we would need a house. Her family offered us their gorgeous carriage house on 77th Street between Park Avenue and Madison Avenue. We accepted. Because I had my own construction team for my development projects, we knew we could renovate the building at cost. It was my first shot at designing a place that my family would live in.

We turned the carriage house into an atrium with a big garden, built a triplex in front of the carriage house and a two-story apartment in the rear, all above an eight car family garage. We lived in the triplex and rented the apartment to cover the property's monthly costs. The idea and the construction crew were mine, but the property and the money we used to redevelop it came from Cornie's family. I loved the new home and was proud of my work, and learned to appreciate the generosity of my wife's family during this transitional time. Part of me wanted to sell my real estate for a loss just so I'd have a little cash to throw into the pot, but whenever I brought up that idea, Cornie readily squashed it. She knew the right move was to wait out the recession.

In addition to working with me, Cornie was fulfilling her career dream of becoming a social worker. Her family has deep ties, going back to the founding of this country. Her great-great-grandfather was among the signers of the Declaration of Independence and the family name was significant both on Wall Street and socially.

Among their many legacies was founding the New York Society for the Prevention of Cruelty to Children (NYSPCC) in 1875, the world's first child protection agency. The NYSPCC offered her a job on its board of directors, but she turned them down. Cornie wanted to be hands-on and became a caseworker for children from troubled families in Harlem, instead. It was one of the most dangerous jobs in New York, because she was dealing with children born into drug-riddled or gangster-run families. I tried my best to convince her to quit the job, but she is fearless, stubborn, and proud. Only when we decided to start a family did she end her social work career.

Cornie gave birth to our daughter Heather in 1973. I was still working for the Kennedy family, a job I couldn't afford to lose. I was still paying back my loans. In any event, the ability to toss around the Kennedy name was too valuable an asset to give up. Cornie took care of everything I couldn't get to—even ordering all the construction materials and dealing with the plumbers and electricians. She really helped maintain and grow the real estate business.

However, by 1974, my working two jobs became too much for the family to handle. I was rarely home and the paltry sum of money I was earning from the Kennedy job was not worth the stress it placed on us. I finally resigned from the office to give my full attention to the real estate projects. Steve Smith smiled when I told him, and the Kennedy office replaced me with Joe Hakim, who went on to enjoy an illustrious career with them. Hakim was actually more qualified for that job than I was and became an invaluable asset to the Kennedys. In fact, he is credited with saving the Merchandise Mart. He was an accountant and when he analyzed the Mart's operation, he learned that it was being so severely mismanaged that if something wasn't done, it would go bankrupt, financially ruining the Kennedy family. His insight saved the Kennedy family, and he later orchestrated the sale of the Merchandise Mart.

Cornie gave birth to our second child, Cori, in 1975, which meant more financial pressure on me. Our family was growing, but my real estate business was not.

Stressed out from financial worries, I arrived at the Piping Rock Beach Club late one summer afternoon, where Cornie was seated at a beach table with golf friends. I sidled up to the bar and ordered a Southside, a deliciously refreshing vodka drink that goes down way too smoothly. I gulped the first one, which calmed my nerves immensely, then ordered a second and leaned back in my chair. I took a deep breath of the ocean air, and thought, "This is going to be a great night."

My moment of zen didn't last long. Seconds after I finished my drink, some trust-fund baby from the club plopped down next to me. His very presence annoyed me. There I was, busting my ass every day of the week, praying to turn my business ventures into a liquid profit, and he was born rich. He'd be financially set forever, even if he never worked another day in his life. The jealousy raged within me. I knew who he was, but didn't really know him. However, I knew that I didn't like him ... in fact, I think I hated him. Then he gave me a reason to hate him even more.

He introduced himself and asked in a condescending voice, "So, what do you do?" I took a sip of my drink and clenched my jaw, trying to maintain my composure, knowing he was purposely trying to get under my skin. He knew who I was. We had met at my wedding. He also knew damn well what I did for a living. He was asking because he thought that working in the construction business meant I was below him socially and he wanted to remind me of that. I didn't want to give him the satisfaction of knowing he was getting to me. If I ignored him, maybe he'd walk away, but he continued his digs. He looked at my crooked boxing fingers with dirt under the nails from a recent visit to one of my construction sites, and said, "You must collect trash?"

"No," I said through a clenched jaw, "actually, I renovate buildings that I own."

"What exactly does that mean?" he asked in the same demeaning tone. I was ready to knock him on his arrogant ass! Then, the phone at the bar rang. The bartender said it was for me. My unwelcomed companion was saved by the bell, or so I thought.

It was Sarasy and he had bad news. My building on West 11th Street was about to be demolished because the city deemed it a fire hazard. I was busy bringing it up to code, but the city did not think the work was moving fast enough. Fire hazards are taken very seriously by the city. Buildings there are erected with little space in between each one; if one catches fire, the entire block could go up in flames.

This was trouble. If the city demolished my building, my investment would go up in flames. Normally, after receiving such a call, I would have met with someone in City Hall and used my influence with the Kennedys to buy more time to bring the building up to code. But I was an hour from both the building and from City Hall and it was late Friday afternoon. There was no possible way for me to get to either in time to make a deal. I asked Sarasy if he could take care of it. He said he'd try and would get back to me as soon as possible. I hung up the phone, trembling in anger and fear that the city might tear down my building and cost me a fortune.

That's when the trust-fund baby started in with me again.

"Was that a construction call?" he asked, stressing the word construction in a nasally and demeaning way.

I'd had it. I told him that if he said one more word to me, I was going to throw my drink in his face or deck him. Of course, he opened his mouth to speak. The expression on his face told me everything I needed to know. Before he could get a word out, I tossed my drink in his face and stood eye to eye with him, daring him to do something about it, making it clear that he was the weak one. He did nothing, and I strutted away, chest puffed out, feeling like a tough guy.

That feeling of superiority lasted only as long as the adrenaline rush. Afterward, I felt pathetic. I was a grown man acting like a schoolyard bully. Yes, he purposely pushed my buttons, but that was one of those incidents where walking away would have made me the bigger man. Fighting is for self-defense and for those few occasions when two men feel the need to test their physical dominance against each other. That trust-fund baby was not challenging me to a physical fight. He was challenging me to a mental war, and because I snapped at him, he won. He was trying to bother me, and I allowed him to do so. I threw the drink in his face because I felt weak, and demeaning him might let me feel like a man again. I had a wife and two children to support, yet I couldn't even support myself. It angered me to be surrounded by men who were financially independent without ever having had to work hard.

Sarasy was able to convince the building inspector to give me more time, and he saved the building. More important, shortly after this incident, my wife, Cornie, indirectly reminded me of an old and valuable lesson that saved my sanity.

But first, some quick background on real estate for context. In New York City, a law called "rent control" was passed in the 1940s after World War II to protect tenants from losing their apartments as a result of rapidly rising rents. Only very small increases are allowed, designed to be small enough to keep tenants from being forced out of their homes. And tenants must be told in advance that their rents will be raised. Anybody purchasing a building with tenants in New York will likely have to deal with rent control—and this can create real financial issues, especially when the costs of owning a building increase far greater than the rents being collected.

When a building goes up for sale, rent control can become a nightmare for the new owner, if they pay too much. Very often, the amount of rent paid doesn't even begin to cover the costs of the mortgage. And rent control prohibits the new owner from raising the rent enough to cover the difference, making the newly purchased property a losing proposition from day one. In such circumstances, if an owner wants to sell a building, he can't ask for market value because any reasonably smart purchaser would do the simple math and realize that the below-market rents mean he will never be able to recoup his investment solely from the rental proceeds. If a prospective buyer is a good negotiator, he stands to make a financial windfall off such a purchase. The goal for a savvy buyer, therefore, is to:

1. Buy the building cheap and then try to offer the tenants a buyout—that is, pay them enough money so that they will agree to end their leases and move someplace else, allowing the new buyer to sign new tenants at any new, market rent price he can collect (rent control does not apply to new leases).

2. Sell the buyout apartments as cooperatives, or co-ops. A co-op is an arrangement whereby the owner sells shares of a building to tenants. In exchange for the share, the tenant is entitled to a housing unit in the property. The deal is similar to a condo, except that the owner of the building never relinquishes his rights as the overall property owner. To convert an apartment building into a co-op, New York law at the time stipulated that two-thirds of the renters had to agree to the change. This stipulation was also meant to protect the renters from being forced out if the owner wanted to convert. To make the conversion to a co-op simple, it was often best for the owner to try to buy out at least two-thirds of the renters and then provide cheap and short-term leases to friends (called "missionaries"), who would then vote in the owner's favor to convert the units into cooperatives. Missionaries would then move out of their own accord, leaving the

owner with an unencumbered building—free of tenants or other owners—which could easily be converted to a co-op, with shares sold at whatever price the market would allow.

Converting buildings into co-ops took masterful negotiating skills. I was arrogant and thought I could easily get it done. Then, I fell in love with four "mixed-use" buildings on 11th Street in Greenwich Village and was quickly humbled.

Despite my difficult financial situation, I felt compelled to purchase the buildings. The location was prime and the price was right. A bank assured me that because I had a strong portfolio and was up-to-date on all my payments, they could provide me with a loan. I met with several of the tenants and came to a fair buyout price. The only family with whom I could not reach an agreement owned a lease on a restaurant in the building as well as two full floors above the restaurant. I could not get the family to agree to sell because they lived in Rome. They owned the restaurant but no longer ran its day-to-day operations, and they left the apartments vacant. What made this situation unique was that the Italian family was also the family selling the four buildings. They were willing to sell the buildings but wouldn't give up their leases. The reason was simple. They had signed long-term leases charging them monthly rent of only $1!

I purchased the buildings anyway, figuring it was only a matter of time before I could contact the family and negotiate a buyout. For the next two years, I sent the Italian renters numerous letters, asking and then begging them to get back to me. They never responded. Their $1 a month rent became too much of a financial burden for me to shoulder. Not only did it ensure I couldn't earn enough rent money to cover my costs, but also I couldn't sell the buildings at market price for a profit (no one else would buy a building with locked in $1 leases and I wanted to sell the buildings as a block, not individually). Nor could I convert the buildings into co-ops until all leases were bought out.

I had to track the family down. I drafted a contract with a $15,000 buyout for the two units and told my wife to pack her bags. We arranged for our live-in nannies to watch the children for two weeks, and Cornie and I were off to Italy to conduct business. The Italian family knew I was coming. I had their attorney, Emanuel Popolizio, contact them earlier in the week and inform them of my pending arrival.

I knocked on the door and an old woman opened it a tiny crack. I explained that I was the American who purchased their old buildings and I showed her the contract. She rambled in Italian for a few moments. I don't speak a word of Italian, but I got the message. When she was done talking, she violently slammed the door in my face. I concluded this meant that she wouldn't be signing the contract.

I turned to Cornie, saying, "I have no idea what to do." And with that twinkle in her eyes that meant "listen carefully to what I am saying," she instructed me: "Buy her flowers."

I thought it was a foolish plan. How could buying that old wretch flowers help me seal a deal? In any case, her family had made my life miserable. Why did they deserve a present? Cornie was adamant that flowers would help. I had nothing to lose, so I ran a few blocks into the town square, purchased a bouquet, and returned to the house. I again knocked on the door and when the old woman opened it a crack to yell at me, I thrust the bouquet into her hands. Doing so forced her to take her hands off the door and allowed Cornie and me to push it open, confront her face to face, and negotiate with her. She had no choice but to talk to us.

She spoke a little English, enough for us to discuss a possible deal. And when negotiations were over, she again said no. Crushed, I handed her the contract and told her that if she changed her mind to call her attorney.

Cornie and I spent a few more days in Rome and then went on to Austria. We toured Vienna and had a great time sightseeing. We then traveled to San Anton to ski. The highlight of that particular trip was the day Cornie (once an Aspen ski instructor) and me skied with an Austrian ski instructor named Hans, who was leading a group around the snowy mountain terrain. He jumped off a ridge and looked up and watched the four skiers ahead of us crash into mounds of snow in front of him. He looked at the two of us Americans, now on the ledge, and said in broken English, "Follow me."

Cornie looked down, shouted "Screw you" to Hans, and skied a different route down to join the group. What memories!

At the end of the week we boarded a plane home, where all I had to return to was a recession-riddled city and an apartment building I couldn't afford to hold on to. But there was a message waiting for me in New York from the Italian family's attorney—they had signed the contract! After showing it to their attorney, he suggested they take the $15,000 buyout. I immediately filled the apartments with my friends ("missionaries") and had them vote to turn the units into cooperatives.

I was out of trouble, and I owed it all to Cornie. This time, however, my pride wasn't bruised. My wife's idea taught me a lesson—we were a team! I was no longer on my own. I was part of something greater. It reminded me of how I'd defeated Johnny Canaan in the ring so many years before. I didn't win that fight on my own; I did it with my brother's help. If I hadn't listened to Cornie, I would never have convinced the family to sign the contract. More important, if I had not learned to accept Cornie as my partner, I might very well have lost her.

Before I could truly appreciate what a great life partner Cornie was, I first had to appreciate what a great a business partner she could be. She was not supporting my business to demean me or because she felt forced. She did it because she loved me and believed in me—and because it was fun and challenging for her. Now that I had her as a partner, I was finally able to pursue my career and increase my capital significantly.

In the late 1970s, the recession ended and my buildings and co-ops could be sold at market value, allowing me to pay off the majority of my loan debt while earning a very nice profit. I had the liquid assets to support my family. I felt like a man again.

I held on to a few properties that together had substantial and stable values, assets against which I could take out future bank loans if needed. I had the best of both worlds—cash and property—which made me a prime target for various investment groups in the city. I received daily calls from developers who wanted me to invest in their properties. The biggest offer came in 1978, when I was offered the opportunity to purchase a $20 million residential development in New York known as Kips Bay.

Kips Bay comprised more than 1,000 rental apartments (mostly rent controlled), occupying two city blocks between 32nd and 35th Streets. I was introduced to the deal by Mayor Robert Wagner's assistant counsel Bernard Ruggieri, a friend of Steve Smith, from the Kennedy office. It was an opportunity for me to become a major developer in Manhattan and be part of big-time Manhattan real estate circles.

"You want to be my partner or buy the building?" the owner of the building asked me, in her Israeli-English accent as we toured the building's basement. "How much money do you have in your bag?" No one had ever asked me that directly.

I wanted to buy the whole damned thing, and I told her I would put $2 million down, almost all of my cash, and pay the rest over for the course of many years. I was riding high on my recent wave of success and was ready to do it, but Cornie put her foot down. "You're out of your goddamn mind," she said. "If you buy that you'll be right back where you were a few years ago—fighting those rent-controlled tenants. Except, instead of a few dozen tenants, you'll have to deal with over 1,000 and it will drive you crazy!"

There was a time I might have argued with her and explained why it was such a great investment. But I had come to respect and honor her opinion on these matters. I knew that for any business venture of mine to succeed, we needed to tackle it as a team. I needed her full support. To this day, she's my emotional partner and we do things as a team or not at all. So I never did buy into that deal, and how lucky for me that I avoided the "opportunity," because there were far better and more exciting things ahead that I would have missed—specifically, my life in Florida.

Our tie to Florida was Black Island. Five years after I invested in the property, we were still trying to complete the development, looking to turn the equivalent of Gilligan's Island into Captiva Island. We had zoning issues and animal, wildlife, and mosquito-control problems. We had to fight environmentalists who wanted to stop the development and preserve the natural integrity of the place. These preservationists pressured the state to buy the land. And, as in any project of substantial magnitude, we had numerous construction problems. I believed in the island's potential, as did Cornie, and thank God she did, because the island took me away from home every month.

Sometimes I'd be gone for only a day or two. Other times I'd be gone for a week or two. My children, ages three and four at the time, were growing up without me and my wife was raising them on her own. The deeper we got into the development process, the more I was away from home and the more Cornie and I were growing apart. This was not an acceptable family situation. We had two solutions:

1. I could ask my partners to buy me out and abandon the project.
2. We could move to Florida.

Cornie agreed to move to Florida. She believed in Black Island. She knew it was a sound investment and would earn us a profit in time. She also favored the idea of leaving New York behind because she felt it was best for the children. She believed that her family's influence and name in New York would have made it impossible for the children to grow up as individuals. She wanted people to see them for themselves, not for who their family and ancestors were.

If Cornie had told me to sell, I would have. Our marriage was more important to me than the money. As difficult as it was for me to accept, when it came to Cornie, I realized more and more that I could not succeed on my own. I needed her in my corner. My plan was to relocate the family to Black Island. I owned part of the island and I wouldn't have to travel far to do business. Cornie, however, was having no part of that plan. She could not see moving the family from the hustle and bustle of New York to a small, mosquito-ridden island with nothing to do. I was upset at her refusal. We'd have to find a reasonable compromise, find a part of Florida where we both wanted to live.

We agreed to take a sightseeing trip through the state to explore the different cities where we could make our home. To me, Miami was fake, a wannabe New York, with palm trees and shallow people we wanted to avoid. Fort Myers was too quiet. Orlando was too touristy, and Sarasota was too small. It was in Sarasota, however, that we learned of Tampa.

Shortly after, we visited some of the homes for sale in Tampa, and fell in love with one located on the seventh hole of a golf course in Carrollwood, North Tampa. We bought it on sight. A few weeks later, we were there with our two children, starting a new and exciting chapter in our lives.

Dick's family, when he was young: father, Donald Sr., brother David (on father's lap), brother Don, Dick, and sister Kathy on mother Margaret's lap

Dick (left) in the ring as a young man

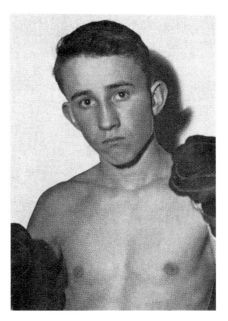

Dick as a teenager with his boxing gloves

Dick and President Dwight D. Eisenhower at the University of Notre Dame

Photo: © University of Notre Dame

Dick, Vice-President Richard Nixon, and the University of Notre Dame's President, Father Theodore Hesburgh

Dick and then-Presidential candidate John F. Kennedy at the University of Notre Dame

Photo: © University of Notre Dame

Dick (center) and Robert F. Kennedy

Alaska trip—Dick and Tampa friends

Aspen ski trip with family: daughters Lamara (far left) and Alyda, wife Cornie (center), son Rick, Dick and daughter, Heather

Dick and Cornie quail hunting at Pinkney Hill

Dick and Cornie

Photo: © Tom Sullivan

14

Only an Idiot Would Purchase a Lease on Land Owned by a Federal Airport

Hello, my name is Dick Corbett, and I am an idiot.

The land I leased is the site of what became one of Tampa, Florida's most successful real estate development projects, where the fabulously successful International Plaza stands today. It's one of the most impressively developed plots of land in the southeastern United States, and it is the real estate project I am most proud of. It includes almost 2.5 million feet of buildings, an office park, a hotel, and a large upscale mall with more than 200 stores and restaurants. And all of it is located right next door to the Tampa International Airport, a mile away from the Tampa Bay Buccaneers' football stadium and the New York Yankees' Steinbrenner spring training facility. And it has been a great success.

But the project's ultimate success does not change the fact that I was an idiot for wanting to develop on land owned by a federal airport. Several times along the way of the project's coming to fruition, I almost lost everything. There were likely easier routes to large-scale development that I could have taken, but I was arrogant, believing that I knew enough, that I had the right contacts, and that the time was just right for me to make this project a success. But largely because of my arrogance, my family and I suffered through more than two decades of development hell, coming close to financial ruin on a number of occasions.

The story of the land next to the Tampa International Airport began during World War II. The federal government took over the airport during the war and later deeded 30 acres of the tract back to the local government, stipulating that the property could be used only for a public airport. In addition, the land could not have tall buildings, which might pose a threat to low-flying planes, and the rent the Tampa Airport Authority collected had to be used for airport improvements. So the land sat vacant for many years because developers could not come up with a use for the land that could turn a profit and still be used by the airport.

In 1961, Jim Walter stepped up to the plate. Walter was one of the most prominent and well-known businessmen in Tampa, the kind of man I most respected—self-made to the bone. A World War II veteran, he returned from the war with only a few hundred dollars to his name and started a trucking company. He diversified his business portfolio in the 1950s, when he purchased his first shell home for $395, fixed it up, and sold it for a profit of $300. He used the profit to purchase another home, fixed that up, turned a bigger profit, and continued to grow. By 1961, he was a self-made millionaire and looking to invest in something really big. The airport's 30 acres of land was as big as it got—undeveloped land sitting right next to a major international airport.

Yes, not only were Walter and I both self-made men—he was also a fellow idiot for wanting that land.

The airport could not sell the land, so a developer would have to negotiate a long-term lease to make building on it worthwhile. No reasonable person was going to spend millions of dollars erecting buildings and building infrastructure for a lease that might run only a few years. The massive investment required a long-term lock on rights to the land.

Walter's idea for the land was to build a motel. The airport had finally grown to a size that could support such a venture, so he erected the Tampa Airport Motel, a small development with only 100 rooms. It didn't seem like a big moneymaking venture, but Walter was looking to the future, not the present. Building that motel meant he had a leg up on future land negotiations with the airport. He wanted to expand his empire on that land.

In the early 1970s, the expansion began. He enlarged the motel to 200 rooms. In 1972, another 40 years and 110 acres were added to Walter's lease. He built a golf course and tennis courts, developments that the Tampa Airport Authority agreed enhanced the airport. Airport officials believed such facilities would lure the small, private jets that the rich businessmen used for traveling away from the

St. Petersburg-Clearwater Airport to the Tampa International Airport. They could stay at the hotel and spend their free time golfing.

From this vision, the Tampa Airport Resort Golf and Racquet Club was born. Walter was flying high. The resort was an instant success. Its motto was "Get away from it all, right here in the middle of it." Businessmen flocked to it for daytime golf and tennis meetings. Celebrity golf tournaments were an annual staple and included such participants as Bear Bryant, Don Shula, Johnny Bench, John McKay, Mickey Mantle, Stan Musial, Pete Rose, and many more, all of whom stayed at the hotel during their visits to Tampa. It became a celebrity-viewing hotspot for the residents of Tampa. Its convenient location near the airport also made it a marital cheating hotspot. Men would tell their wives they had business out of town, leave their cars at the airport in case their suspicious wives checked up on them, and take a cab to the motel to meet their girlfriends for a weekend getaway—golfing by day and womanizing by night. The motel staff was carefully selected and well trained; they were instructed never to divulge the names of the guests using the motel, to avoid scandals.

Walter continued to wheel and deal. He subleased a plot of land to the Tampa Bay Buccaneers, who built the team headquarters and a training facility on it. The Buc players stayed at the motel during training camp, furthering the popularity of the resort. During the Bucs preseason, the resort was *the* place to be for football fans. They would play a round of golf, watch the Bucs practice, and grab a beer and a steak at the resort's restaurant.

Despite all of these successes, by the mid- to late 1970s, Walter wanted out. The Federal Aviation Authority was a thorn in his paw, constantly complaining that his rent was too low and that the golf course interfered with FAA radar. He also realized that while he could continue to turn a small profit off the land, it would never be enough to justify the amount of work it took to run the operation. Unfortunately, the airport would not rezone the land so that he could build anything that could yield a larger profit. Walter was not in the business of playing political games with the federal government or the county; he was interested only in making money.

In the late 1970s, Walter's wife was diagnosed with cancer. He was no longer willing to battle with the airport. He decided to sell his lease. To do so, he needed to find a big enough boob to take it off his hands. That boob was me, arriving in 1978 to make my fortune in Tampa.

I was semi-retired when we arrived in Tampa. I was managing existing properties, but I was retired from developing new projects. The money I made off my real estate in New York was sufficient to allow me to sit back and enjoy life for a while. Throw in Cornie's savings and our family had no financial worries. The only projects I had on my plate were a few New York brownstones I held onto and Black Island, which took about a week or so of my time each month.

I spent most of my first few months driving the children to school, reading the newspaper, and checking up on my real estate and Cornie's stocks and bonds. I would play golf and visit the beach from time to time, the things retired people are supposed to do. Retired at age 40! Fantastic! Relaxing! A dream come true!

And so utterly *boring.*

I'm not the retirement type. I need to be active, to be hustling, to be neck deep in development deals. I was going stir crazy. I was going through withdrawal.

Making money is only half the reason I love the world of real estate and development. I also crave the excitement of the risks, the negotiations, the bluffing, the multimillion-dollar deals. It was the thrill of the hunt and the joy of the kill that drove me, always trying to leave the room with the bigger part of the stick. Then there's the excitement of working to make the development a success—tracking down tenants in Italy, haggling with contractors over restoration prices, modifying loans. Being in the midst of a deal or trying to turn a flawed development into a financial windfall was so exciting it made my head buzz. It still gives me a high.

In semiretirement, I no longer had that high, and I missed it.

After three or four months of that boredom, I was pulled out of retirement by my neighbor, Ben Norbom, a real estate broker and apartment manager. He told me he had a sweet deal on some apartments in Orlando that had been foreclosed on by the St. Petersburg Savings and Loan. If I could buy the property, he could manage the place and we could both earn a profit. He was right. It was a great deal. I analyzed the hell out of the apartment complex's financial particulars and could not find a scenario that could lose us money. I was in! Alive again! But it would not be easy.

The bank wanted the mortgage to be bought outright for $2.1 million, but no way was I going to part with that much cash. We had to convince the bank to modify the mortgage and sell it to me according to what I could afford—$100,000 down and the rest paid off in monthly installments. A negotiating process like that usually takes months. We did it in days.

My attorney for the deal was Stella Ferguson Thayer. Bronson and Stella Thayer were not only our first friends in Tampa, they quickly became two of our closest friends. Stella was someone I could trust and a well-qualified attorney. I sent her the information on the apartment complex mortgage and asked if she could help negotiate a deal. She read it over and got back to me within an hour, proclaiming she could do more than help. She could get it done immediately. As it turned out, her father was close friends with the chairman of the board of the bank holding the mortgage. She explained that if I wanted that mortgage, all I had to do was convince her father that it was a good business deal.

Stella's father was Chester Ferguson, also known as "Mr. Tampa," the most powerful and influential man in the city, so powerful that George Steinbrenner, the Boss himself, called him "Big Daddy." Ferguson fought in WWII in the Army Air Corps, where he was awarded, among other honors, the air medal and the bronze star. He returned from war and excelled as a public defender before branching out into the private legal sector. He was an early partner in Macfarlane and Ferguson, which quickly became one of the state's premiere law firms. He was also the first chairman of the Florida Board of Regents; chairman of the board of directors and CEO of First Florida Bank Corporation; and chairman of the board of directors and CEO of Lykes Brothers, Inc., Tampa's most powerful corporation at the time, boasting huge assets in shipping, cattle, meat packing, citrus, banking, utilities, electronics, and steel. In short, the Lykes Brothers was a great influence on Tampa and Ferguson ran Lykes Brothers. Everyone knew Ferguson and everyone respected him. If you had him on your side, you could accomplish just about anything in Tampa.

He agreed that the apartment building was a good deal and said he would help. He said he did indeed know the chairman of the board of the bank. He picked up the telephone and arranged for us to meet 45 minutes later.

When we got to the bank he told me to stay in the foyer while he talked to his friend Raleigh Green, the chairman of St. Petersburg Savings and Loan. Five minutes later, Ferguson returned to the foyer and said, "You need to pay the bank $25,000 in cash for them to modify the mortgage, which it will do with a quarter point increase in the interest rate, along with the $100,000 down payment." He got me the deal, and all he had to do was vouch for me. The bank would have accepted any deal I threw at them, as long as Ferguson was behind it. Tampa was no different from New York. All I had to do was replace the Kennedy name with the Ferguson name, and I became one of the most well-connected men in the city. With Ferguson on my side, even the sky was not the limit. I later sold the apartment complex for a multimillion-dollar profit.

In the months that followed that deal, I invested in an apartment complex in Gainesville and an office building in Jacksonville, both on broker Norbom's advice. I was fully out of retirement, and it was no different from what I'd been doing in New York. Still, it was getting a little boring.

After making the same deal and using the same process to make the deal work, time and time again, the routine was beginning to get dull. I was working again, but the spark was missing, the challenge was gone. This is a common experience for developers. That's why we're always investing in larger and larger projects and pushing our finances to the brink of bankruptcy. We crave the high! It's like any drug—you have to continue to do more and more to feel it.

So when I learned of Jim Walter's 140 acres of land next to the airport I got excited again. I wanted that land; it was something new and completely different. I didn't see a motel and golf course. I saw far greater potential; indeed, I believed the land was the most valuable in the city. With 140 acres right next to an international airport, the possibilities were limitless. I wanted to bulldoze the entire property and start from scratch. I wanted to put out an unprecedented call to developers across the nation: come build on land located right next to an international airport, on which I own the lease. I envisioned top developers from around the world flocking to my office to negotiate with me. I would charge them all a king's ransom to develop the land. The lease was so affordable that I would make a fortune off subleasing to the others.

I knew Walter was giving the land up because he couldn't get it zoned for anything other than its current use, but that didn't faze me. I was arrogant and wildly self-confident. I figured that with the negotiation skills I'd honed throughout my years of dealing with tenants in rent-controlled apartment complexes, I could succeed where Walter had failed. Plus, I knew Chester Ferguson.

But Ferguson didn't want me to get involved with the airport land. He thought it was a quicksand business deal, a financial death trap. The more I struggled to survive, he warned, the quicker I would sink. Never develop federally owned land, he said. The government is impossible as a landlord or a partner. But I wouldn't budge. I wanted the lease and persisted doggedly. Despite his reservations, Ferguson put the airport lease deal together for me. He called Walter, set up the meeting, and we came to an agreement. I would purchase the lease for the 140 acres for $5 million and begin making the monthly payments to the airport immediately.

Ferguson called the airport's attorney to pressure him into rezoning the land for me, but his efforts failed. I'm not sure if Ferguson had ever been rebuffed before. He slammed the phone down and screamed, "That damn pinhead!"

If the most powerful man in the city couldn't make a deal happen, how could I? Most men would have given up, but I wouldn't back down. I was pigheaded and overconfident, Ferguson pointed out. He laughed at me, saying apparently no one could get the airport to rezone that land and voiced again his belief that I would be getting in way over my head. But I followed my intuition, knowing that there was a high risk. His cautions just served to embolden me. I wanted to prove him wrong. Maybe he knew me better than I knew myself and planted the seed of impossibility to egg me on, knowing that I would come out fighting and find a way to win.

Ferguson continued to back my dream. He took me to First Florida Bank, one of 17 banks that fell under the Lykes family empire, and introduced me to the bank's senior executive vice president, Jim Warren. He told Warren I had a good asset deal and should be given the loan. It worked, of course, and I used that money to purchase the lease from Walter. I became the official owner of the lease and the resort sitting on that property.

I still had one more issue to address. I didn't know a thing about running an inn, hotel, or motel. I needed a partner who did. I reached out to my old friend and mentor, Lew Sarasy, and he recommended John McGuire, a friend of his in Wisconsin who owned a number of Holiday Inns. Sarasy trusted him, but I decided against a partnership. It was a gut reaction. A business acquaintance in Tampa suggested that I partner with Bill Graulich, a New Jersey–based businessman who owned a few Holiday Inns across the country and who was president of the United States Holiday Inn Franchise Operators

Association. He was a bigger name than McGuire, so I figured he was the better partner. Graulich and I agreed that he would run the hotel and I would run the golf course. What did I know about running a golf course? Nothing. But running one business I knew nothing about was better than running two.

On July 31, 1979, the deal was official. I was part-owner of a 140-acre land lease.

Following every high comes a crash.

It turned out Ferguson was right. I was in way over my head, and things got off to a terrible start. I should have done more due diligence on my hotel partner. He started robbing me blind.

Two months after we took over the resort, I learned that most of the motel's bills were not being paid. I received a call from the electric company, from the water company, from the phone company, and even from the butcher. No one was being paid. And the motel was not showing a profit.

I hired a Laventhol and Horwath accountant to research the matter before I stirred up a hornet's nest. I knew it was best to get all the information before I made any accusations. But someone in the motel tipped off my partner about what I was up to. Graulich called me, demanding to know why I was "sticking my nose in his business." I asked him calmly why he wasn't paying the bills, and he responded, "I run the motel. You run the golf course! Stay out of my business!"

That was it. He was done.

The accountant, was a former Cornell football nose tackle on the gridiron. He was large enough to scare most men with a simple glare. The day after my phone conversation with Graulich, he and I flew to New Jersey to visit Graulich in his office. But my accountant wasn't going to be doing any accounting. He was acting as my backup.

We stormed into Graulich's office, only to be informed he wasn't there. He knew we were coming, probably thought if he disappeared he could deter us. He couldn't have been more wrong. We pushed past his employees, walked into his office, found his box of files on the Tampa airport motel, and walked out—files and all—ignoring the office workers' demands to return them immediately. They were all talk, a bunch of business school graduates who'd never been in a real fight in their lives. None of them was ready to get in my accountant's way. We were playing hardball, New Jersey–style business politics.

We rushed to the airport and Graulich followed us, but he was too late. He arrived just as our Eastern Airlines flight was taking off.

On the flight home, my accountant looked over the files and found all the proof we needed. Graulich was paying the employees and a few bills here and there, skipping most of them, and then depositing the rest of the motel's monthly balance into his account. He was getting rich at the motel's expense. When we landed in Tampa, I immediately called Thayer and told her to meet me at the motel.

When Thayer arrived, I grabbed the motel manager, Clyde Thody, by the shirt, pulled him into the office, sat in the manager's chair, and told him I knew he was in on the whole scam. He denied it, but Thayer informed him that we had the files and his name was all over the receipts. I fired him and told him to call his partner in crime and tell him that I'd see him in court.

The lawsuit was one of the easiest Thayer ever tried, because the evidence was so overwhelming. By the end of 1979, I was the sole owner of the Tampa Airport Resort Golf and Racquet Club and I had learned a valuable lesson: partner only with a man you *know* you can trust. McGuire was a friend of Sarasy, who had vouched for him. I should have called McGuire after my partnership with Graulich fell through and begged for his help, but I was sour on partnerships at that point and decided to make a go of it myself, despite how little I knew about running a motel.

From the start, Cornie was an enormous help. Though she'd never done anything like it in her life, she took over the motel. She was catering to guests, helping with bags, assisting the cleaning crew. Though she had far greater talents, she was essentially doing menial labor. But she loved me and she knew I needed her. Cornie was the soothing voice of ownership of the motel during those stressful early times. If not for her, I don't think the employees would have stuck around. They would not have been able to handle me as their 24/7 boss.

Cornie was one of a trio of amazing women who helped me survive the early years of my airport lease. The other two were Melanie Craig and Jennifer Kent. I met Melanie when she was a teenager working for Jim Fusco in New York. A mountain of a man, at 230 pounds, and a former Cornell football player from Brooklyn, Fusco earned his MBA from Columbia Business School. His appearance was deceptive. At first glance, he seemed like a big, fumbling lummox. But it took only a few moments of speaking with him to realize the depth of his intelligence.

I had met him through the Kennedys' Fort Myers land deal. He was working with an investment firm called Hornblower Weeks Noyes & Trask, which was helping to put the deal together. We always had a great time together. He was a real wild man. On one occasion he stopped by the Kennedy office to see me and whipped out his toothbrush and toothpaste and brushed his teeth in the office water fountain. I'd seen Walsh, the office manager, angry a number of times, but that day he was at his angriest. I thought his head would explode. Fusco and I later partnered in New York on a brownstone that turned a healthy profit. But what made our relationship so important was meeting Melanie.

I was immediately taken by this young, self-educated girl working—indeed thriving—unintimidated in a world of college-educated men. She later earned a degree from Pace College in New York and married a construction superintendent named Steve Gibson, who renovated the Greenwich Village brownstones for me. That's when I got to know Melanie better.

Years later, when Melanie and Steve decided to move to Florida, Fusco did not want her to leave him. She was an invaluable part of his staff. But she'd had enough of the fast-paced New York lifestyle. Her mind was set on Florida. Bad break for Fusco. Good deal for me. I swooped right in and hired her as my office accountant. She would review all my cash flows and financial data and suggest where to make cuts, where to spend more, and where to stand pat, so that the motel would always at least break even. I've met few people in my life with her ability to absorb information and use it to solve puzzles. She can take the most complex situation and break it down into lay-men's terms. She also has a lot of patience, which is essential when dealing with me.

My other office angel was Jennifer Kent. Hers is that sweet British voice that's been representing my office on the phone since 1980. She has the perfect demeanor for a front office. People would rather meet at my office than in a five-star restaurant, just because they want to say hello to Jennifer.

Before moving to Tampa, Jennifer was a human resource specialist with the British embassy in Washington, DC. As her term was ending, she was asked by a consultant to help with a hotel project in Tampa. I then purchased the property, and after seeing how well she managed things, I asked her to stay. Jen has worked with me ever since and I don't think I could remember to tie my own shoes without her. It's not easy being my assistant. My head is often everywhere but on my shoulders. She's the one who keeps me in check, makes sure I never miss an appointment, and lectures me when I fall behind in any work-related assignments.

One of the secrets to my success is having a knack for surrounding myself with people who excel in the areas in which I'm weak. I sometimes overlook the minute details that are so important to a project's financial well-being, which is what Melanie is good at. If I were a child in today's world, I would definitely be diagnosed with attention deficit disorder. I've had a hard time keeping my life in order, which is what Jennifer is good at.

Having three fabulously competent and loyal women helping me to run the day-to-day operations of my business freed me up to search for ways to get the land rezoned. My first big break came courtesy of the motel's restaurant. Because it was located right next to the airport, many of the airport's employees frequented it for meals. One of our best customers was George Bean, the airport's executive director. I buddied up to him right away and made sure my staff treated him with the utmost respect. The restaurant manager, Doris Edwards, always prepared Bean's favorite breakfast, Wheaties with sliced strawberries and bananas with cream. Throw in a little extra coffee and the airport manager was a happy man at 7 a.m.

I would sit down with him and talk sports, politics, and family. And I always ended our time together with a pitch for getting the land rezoned. He would not budge. But in the early 1980s, he provided me with a clever idea. "Give this place a sports theme. You have a golf course, and you have the Bucs. Maybe rebranding it a sports-themed hotel would make it a destination for local sports fans to watch the games and for out-of-towners to stay at when they come to see the games."

I followed his advice. I had to. I was desperate. If things didn't turn around soon, I was going to lose everything. I mean everything! I had put up all my assets to get the loan for the lease. Soon the Tampa Airport Resort Golf and Racquet Club was no more. It became the Hall of Fame Inn. I adorned it with sports collectibles and touted it as Tampa's only sports resort run by a Tampa sports franchise owner. Yes, you read that correctly—by that time Cornie and I owned a professional sports team.

CHAPTER 15

I Will Be Forever Grateful That I Injured My Back and Ribs

I injured my back in my early twenties. I was a nobody at the time—a kid fresh out of Harvard, working for the Kennedy family, looking to toss the Kennedy name around as often as possible to open doors of opportunity. Several of my colleagues, Dennis and Andrew Barber and Larry Lavan, all very well-to-do young men, invited me to go horseback riding with them in Winchester County one weekend.

There was one problem with this invite: I could barely ride a horse! I had ridden on a handful of occasions at most and I should have told my friends the truth. But horseback riding was considered an upper-class activity and I was afraid I'd appear to be below them on the economic food chain if I confided that I was a novice at the sport. It always goes back to wearing that emotional costume. I felt I needed to impress everyone, convince them that I came from an emotionally and economically stable family. So when my friends asked me if I could ride, I said, "Of course."

Riding horses is, well, hard. There's no way you can pretend to be good at it. I was skilled enough to maintain my balance and direct the horse if it stayed calm. But if it rebelled, I was going to be in trouble. Our journey started off calmly. My friends led me through some country trails that were easy to navigate. The horse they loaned me was obeying my every command. I thought I was going to make it through the day without them realizing I was a complete fraud. I thought wrong.

The country trail was briefly interrupted by a roadway. All we had to do was cross the road and enter the trail on the other side. It should have been nothing more than a temporary diversion, a few seconds' trek. It ended up causing me a lifetime of problems. As my horse's hooves touched down on the pavement, a car ahead of us roared its engine and spooked my ride. The horse reared up, a common defense to threats. Any experienced rider would have dug his feet into the horse's side, grabbed the reigns sternly, and ordered the horse to calm down. The key word is *experienced*. Having no idea what to do, I froze; rather than controlling the horse, I allowed the horse to control me. I was tossed from the saddle and landed on the concrete, injuring my lower back in three places.

I've had severe pain in that part of my body ever since. Athletic activities that involve short and quick movements have become more difficult to do over the years. Even golf became challenging. Successfully driving the ball off the tee hinges on a quick twist of the back, an activity that was often too painful for me. But one thing I could do pain free was hit short shots. Although you're supposed to twist your back when hitting short shots, I developed a stroke that allowed me to keep my back straight and still reach my target. Rather than forcing myself to work on my painful long drives, I spent much of my time working on my pain-free short game and mastered it.

Golf became one of my three favorite sports, the others being bird shooting and skiing, a sport that actually improved my golf game in a roundabout manner. For many years, the entire family traveled to Aspen for extended periods to hit the slopes. It was always a wonderful experience—except for the year I broke my ribs. What made the accident so embarrassing was that I didn't break them skiing. I broke them resting. I was at the top of a hill in Aspen, waiting for the kids. I leaned on the side of a ski pole, lost my balance on thin ice, landed awkwardly, and broke a few ribs. To protect the ribs as they healed, I had to wear a thick and constraining flak jacket for about eight weeks.

I refused to allow the broken ribs to lay me up. I continued to ski that weekend and when I returned to Tampa I continued to golf. But playing with a flak jacket proved difficult; it constricted my swing, making it even shorter. Ironically, it turned out to be a blessing. One Saturday morning, I decided to take in 18 holes on my own at Avila Country Club, always a very relaxing pastime. When golfing solo, there's no one rushing your game and no one pressuring you to perform well. My son Rick was with me, but he was all of five or six at the time. He just enjoyed riding in the cart with me and rarely made a peep. I'm glad he was with me; otherwise, no one would have been around to see one of my greatest athletic achievements.

I was on the fifth hole, a par-3, 110-yarder. I was swinging a nine iron. Because I had to concentrate on my swing and move slowly due to my rib injury, I never allowed my eyes to leave the tee. When I connected, I had no idea where it landed. The green was within viewing distance, yet the ball was nowhere to be found. Rick and I rushed over to the green, but the ball wasn't there. He looked in the surrounding rough. No sign of it. The ball was missing. Then Rick peered into the hole. You guessed it. A hole-in-one!

Now, the incredible part: The following day I was playing 18 holes with architect Gerry Curts on the same course. On the 17th hole, I buried yet another hole in one. Two days. Two holes-in-one.

In one of his *Tampa Tribune* newspaper columns, my friend Tom McEwen quoted *Sports Illustrated* saying the odds of anyone hitting two holes in one, two days in a row, was 40 million to 1. Then he quipped, "With Corbett's swing, the odds were even higher."

These experiences will forever be among my favorite stories because they contain a valuable business lesson: if you're tenacious, failure can lead to success. I could have cried myself a river when I realized my back injury would prevent me from mastering my long game. Instead, I mastered the part of the game I could. And I might have cried over my broken ribs and sat on the couch for the eight weeks during recovery. Instead, I stayed active. Both injuries were due to athletic failures, yet both were directly responsible for one of my most notable athletic achievements.

Which brings us back to my years as owner of the Tampa Bay Rowdies, Tampa's professional soccer team. The Rowdies will forever be one of my greatest business failures; the team folded under my family's watch. But without that failure, I might never have become the success I am today.

Ever since I realized that I would not become a professional athlete, I dreamed of doing the next best thing—owning my own professional sports franchise. Of course, what successful businessman doesn't dream of owning his own sports franchise? It's a sexy venture. Among my list of friends who also dreamed of owning a team was Hugh Culverhouse.

In 1972, Culverhouse had a handshake agreement to purchase the Los Angeles Rams for $17 million. The franchise reneged on the deal and instead sold it to Robert Isray for $19 million. Culverhouse was furious and sued the NFL, claiming the franchise was rightfully his. He settled out of court when the NFL promised him first rights to a future expansion franchise. But he turned down an offer to purchase the Seattle Seahawks in 1974. Living in Jacksonville, he was not too keen on uprooting his entire life for the team. In 1976, the NFL offered him a team in Tampa, the Buccaneers, and he agreed to purchase the franchise.

The most important secret to every successful business venture isn't actually much of a secret—supply versus demand. Millions of people fantasize about owning a professional sports franchise. The supply is *very* limited. Culverhouse had one and he knew this meant major dollar signs. He began shopping around for partners, and I was one of the first people to whom he made his pitch.

I had become acquainted with Culverhouse while working on the Black Island deal. He was a powerful Florida attorney who represented quite a few developers with whom I was negotiating to build on the island. He was also a former collegiate boxer, and whenever we were together, we each boasted of our boxing conquests, always trying to outdo the other. We became friends in a short time.

When it comes to business, however, there are few, and most often, no friends. The Buccaneers partnership deal he offered me was ludicrous. The NFL wanted $16 million for the team. Culverhouse told me that he would make me a 50-50 partner for $16 million. Yup. He wanted someone else to purchase the team *and* give him 50-50 partnership. Plus, Culverhouse had to be the face of the ownership partnership. Whoever bought the team had to take a backseat to him.

He knew he would find someone willing to make the deal. There was no telling when another NFL team would be up for sale, and even if it happened again soon, the number of rich businessmen throughout the nation that would bid on it made the chances of winning a team pretty slim—supply versus demand at its finest. Culverhouse had a team and was willing to take on a partner. Those who dreamed of owning a professional sports franchise saw this as their only opportunity, no matter how one-sided the deal was.

I turned him down. I did not have $16 million nor did I want to get a loan for such a deal. Even if I had had $16 million in petty cash stashed in my mattress, I wouldn't have done it. Instead, a businessman from Cincinnati agreed to the terms, and the legend of Hugh Culverhouse was born. Most people think of him as an NFL legend because he was the original owner of the Bucs. Men like me, however, look upon him as a business legend for pulling off that crazy deal.

Another Tampa sports and business icon with whom I was friends was George Steinbrenner. Steinbrenner, of course, owned the New York Yankees, but he also owned American Shipbuilding, which was located in Tampa. Though he was thought to be a New Yorker, he was actually a Tampa resident. I met Steinbrenner through Ferguson shortly after I arrived in Tampa. As we became friends and he spoke about the Yankees, I boiled with jealousy. I often asked him to sell me a portion of the team, but he always said no. He was the majority owner and that's how he wanted to keep it; he wanted all the power and fame. If he sold off too much of the team, he could lose some of that, especially if the partner had a large personality. Plus, partnerships, he would say, are like loveless marriages. Loveless marriages often end in bitter divorces, as do most partnerships, which is why he wanted to remain the primary leader of the Yankees.

My path to sports franchise ownership began with George Strawbridge, a Philadelphia native and resident whose family was the major founder of Campbell's Soup. He used his fortune to purchase the Buffalo Sabres and the Tampa Bay Rowdies. My wife, Cornie, had met Strawbridge years earlier, when they were fox hunting together in Pennsylvania. Later, when we moved to Tampa and lived on the same Carrollwood Golf Course where Strawbridge owned a condo, we would often run together on the golf course for exercise.

By 1979, Strawbridge was growing weary of constantly traveling back and forth between Philadelphia and Tampa. It was a trip he had to make regularly, however, because the fans expected to see the owner of the team at the home games. There was only one solution to Strawbridge's dilemma—sell a portion of the soccer team to a local. While we were out running one day, he offered me 5% ownership of the Tampa Bay Rowdies for $100,000. It sounded like the deal of a lifetime for both of us. He'd have a local to become the face of the franchise, allowing him to cut back on his hectic travel schedule, yet he wouldn't give up control of the team. And I'd fulfill my dream of owning a sports franchise.

At the time, many people thought that purchasing part of an American soccer team sounds funny. It was *soccer*, after all, an afterthought in the American sports landscape. In the 1970s, however, soccer was building steam in the United States. The Tampa

Bay Rowdies were born in 1974, the 16th North American Soccer League (NASL) franchise. The team was an immediate hit in Tampa, both on the field and in the bleachers. The team earned a 16-and-6 record in its inaugural outdoor season, won its division, and won the Soccer Bowl title in front of an average of more than 12,000 home fans per game at Tampa Stadium. In 1978, the Rowdies played before almost 75,000 fans in the title game at the Meadowlands. They lost the game to the New York Cosmos, but the game's unbelievable attendance was a victory on the business field. Soccer was gaining the type of popularity in the United States that it generated around the world. It was a sport on the rise and a business on the rise.

Owning 5% of the team sounded like such a good business venture that my good friends Stella Thayer and Bob Blanchard wanted in on the action. Each wanted to purchase 5% of the team as well. Strawbridge loved the idea, deciding that having three locals owning a part of the team was good public relations.

Our first year as part owners was a resounding success. The team was again league runner-up and averaged close to 29,000 fans per home game. The NASL also had a full 12-game season indoor league that year. The indoor Rowdies enjoyed the same success as the outdoor Rowdies. Using primarily players from the outdoor team, the indoor team won the championship in the inaugural season and sold out almost every game at its indoor arena, the 7,500-seat Bayfront Center in St. Petersburg. We were flying high.

In 1980, attendance remained steady at almost 29,000 per game for the outdoor team and sellouts indoors, but in 1981 the team experienced a hiccup both on the field and in the bleachers. The outdoor team stumbled to a 15-and-17 record and attendance dropped to 22,531. The indoor team finished at 9 and 9, and attendance began to slip as well. In 1982, the outdoor team missed the playoffs for the first time in its history and attendance dropped to an average of 18,500. The outdoor team again missed the playoffs in 1983, finishing 7 and 23, averaging barely over 11,000 fans per game. The indoor team finished as runner-up and was playing in half-packed arenas both at home and on the road. This was not a local trend. Soccer's popularity was fading across the country. I, unfortunately, was blind to that trend. I had missed one of Joe Kennedy's steps to success; I didn't know my market at all.

Following the 1983 season, Strawbridge, with intelligent foresight, offered to sell Thayer, Blanchard, and me the entire team for $2.1 million, $700,000 apiece. He told us his wife was growing weary of the sports franchise business and he had to sell off one of his two teams. Since Buffalo was closer to Philadelphia than Tampa, the Rowdies were the easy choice, he said.

Earlier that year, the state of Florida had bought Black Island for approximately $12 million. The state caved to the demands of the environmentalists, who demanded that the state preserve the land. It wasn't the $20 million I was promised, but I did turn $750,000 into a little over $3.5 million, so I had some money with which to play. Buying a larger ownership percentage of the Rowdies was possible. It was also a necessity.

It was no longer only about ego or owning something as cool as a sports team. It was about survival. I needed the Hall of Fame Inn to prosper if I was going to be able to continue to afford to pay for the lease on the airport's property as I sought ways to rezone the land for larger developments. If the Hall of Fame Inn was going to succeed, I believed I needed to do more than own a sports franchise. I needed to be *the* face of the franchise, not a minority owner. I believed that purchasing name recognition in the sports world would drive sports fans to my establishment.

Thayer, Blanchard, and I thought the team's attendance woes were due to the poor product on the field. We knew the team was having financial problems, but we thought if the team won, it would again attract enormous crowds and become the toast of the town. We were blind to the national trend, blind to the truth—soccer had peaked in the United States. It was a fad that would last only a few years, and Strawbridge knew it. He didn't want to sell the team because he was tired of traveling. He knew the downward spiral was only going to get worse. We had been duped!

We weren't the only ones who didn't see the writing on the wall. Other businessmen actually invested in new soccer leagues—the United States Soccer League (USSL) and the Major Indoor Soccer League (MISL). Each league had to compete for top players and each league won its share of battles. This was a loss for all soccer fans; it was diluting the leagues' talent pool. Games were no longer crisp displays of soccer prowess. With less-talented and fewer big-name players dominating the field, the games were second-rate action.

As attendance continued to drop, player salaries had to be lowered. This caused players to rush back to the European leagues, which were offering higher salaries. Many of the top players who remained did so for only one of the two seasons, either indoor or outdoor, and played the other season in a European League, forcing many of the teams to scramble to fill rosters. Only a handful of top players participated in both seasons.

Quite a few players from the 1983 team were free agents, and we couldn't afford to resign them. Hell, we couldn't afford to sign enough players to fill our 1984 roster, not even players from the bottom of the talent pool. This was an issue for teams throughout the NASL, and league officials were worried that the 1984 season wouldn't happen. They doubted the league could field enough teams.

A few months before the start of the 1984 season, NASL team owners met in New York to discuss the future of the league. Thayer and I attended, armed with ideas for how to turn the league around. We approached owning the team the same as we would any business venture: for any business to survive it needs to change with the times. People in the United States were no longer interested in "classic soccer," so we had to adapt the rules to fit what they wanted to watch. US sports fans like quick, high-scoring games. The rules Thayer and I suggested included things like shortening the field and abandoning offsides.

Some of the owners did not appreciate our ideas. We were the new kids on the block and our take-the-lead attitude with the veteran owners didn't sit well, particularly with the owner of the Chicago team, Lee Stern. "Why don't you shut up!" he spat from across the meeting table. "You don't have any right talking here. Until you've lost the type of money the rest of us have lost, you have no right making suggestions!"

Stern is a business icon, considered one of the greatest commodity traders in the history of the nation, a pit bull in the boardroom. But he wasn't about to intimidate me. "What?" I coolly asked, clenching my fists under the table.

"We've all lost close to $20 million over the past few years," he ranted. "When you lose that type of money, you can talk at a meeting!"

My bulging eyes and clenched jaw told everyone at the table what I thought about Stern's disrespectful attitude. Joe Robbie, owner and founder of both the NFL's Miami Dolphins and the NASL's Miami Strikers, was sitting next to me and tried to calm me. "Dick," he said in a soothing voice, "remain calm."

I ignored the advice. I had never allowed any man to disrespect me in public in my life and I was not about to start. Stern was in his mid-50s and in nowhere near the shape I was in. He was flabby and weak and a hearing aid jutted out of his right ear. There was nothing about him that instilled fear in me. "If that son of a bitch across the table from me talks to me once more that way, I'll smash him with a left hook so hard his hearing aid will go from his right ear to his left!"

The fool opened his mouth to retort. He obviously had no idea the type of man I was.

Before he could mutter a syllable, I leaped from my seat, determined to hurt him. I was going to show off the boxing combinations I'd learned so many years earlier. Luckily for him, Giorgio Chinaglia, the giant Italian soccer star who was playing in the NASL and representing the players at the meeting, was sitting next to me. He grabbed me around the waist and prevented me from caving in Stern's face.

Needless to say, the league was in trouble. Not only were the fans turning away from it; the owners couldn't find a way to work together to improve it. Only one major decision was made at the meetings. Teams would cut their rosters by a few players and teams that were financially stable would loan their excess players to the struggling teams, such as the Rowdies.

Unfortunately, the other teams loaned us their worst players.

Thayer, Blanchard, and I decided to terminate our contract with Tampa Stadium. It was too costly to play there and the games were not drawing the type of attendance we needed to pay the bills. We played instead at the Tampa Fairgrounds Arena, which was half the size of the stadium.

The Tampa Bay Rowdies' 1984 season did not look promising. We continued to try to improve the team, though, hiring the team's most popular former player, Rodney Marsh, as coach. Marsh had played four seasons for the Rowdies, 1976 through 1979, leading the team to league runner-up twice, in 1978 and 1979, and to an indoor title in 1976. He was named team MVP in 1977 and 1978, Most Popular Rowdie in 1977, 1978, and 1979, and was inducted into the Rowdies Hall of Fame in 1982. We hoped that bringing back such a popular and skilled player as coach would result in immediate improvements on the field and in attendance. We were wrong. No matter how much he knew about the game, he needed quality players to win. And no matter how beloved he was in Tampa Bay, people wanted to cheer for a winning team, not the coach.

During our first year as majority owners, the team finished 9 and 14 in the outdoor league, in front of only a few thousand fans per game, and missed the playoffs. When the season was over, the team was financially upside down. We'd lost more than $2 million that season. We could not afford to pay the players' salaries the following season, forcing us to terminate the contracts of the majority of the players. The only players we kept were those whose contracts we could cover by loaning them to European teams. Contracts stated the players could play only for the Rowdies, but for a fee we would ignore that clause and allow them to play elsewhere during our off-season. But I even found a way to screw that up!

Roy Wegerle, an outstanding young man and our best player, was loaned to Chelsea to play in the English Premier League. The owner promised to pay us $250,000 if Wegerle played a required number of games and was successful. Chelsea was smart. The team purposely played him in one less game than was required, thus nullifying the $250,000.

Teams throughout the league were suffering similar financial pains. Some of these owners had had enough. They were tired of losing money and decided to fold their franchises. Unable to field enough teams for the 1985 season, the NASL also folded. I began talking to the MISL and the USSL, hoping to land the Rowdies a spot in either of their upcoming seasons.

Thayer and Blanchard wanted out. They were tired of losing money and did not think a new league would solve the team's financial woes. But I did not want to quit. For my inn to succeed, I still felt I needed the public business image that owning a sports team would provide. I needed the inn to prosper so I could pay the bills on the land as I tried to get it rezoned. Plus, I was convinced there would be light at the end of the tunnel—that my persistence and my no-quit attitude would turn the team around and help feed my larger dreams. I had never quit on an investment in my life.

In 1985, I became the sole owner of the Tampa Bay Rowdies. Thayer and Blanchard agreed to give me their shares if I took on any debt the team had incurred during their ownership. I was the sole provider for the team, a team that was losing money, which meant all expenses had to come out of my pocket.

I wasn't able to come to terms with the MISL or USSL. Without a league to call home, the Tampa Rowdies operated as an independent soccer team in 1985. We toured the nation, playing exhibition games against other independent teams and against teams in established leagues. We also played exhibition games at home at the Tampa Fairgrounds Arena. Unfortunately, barely a thousand people would attend the home games. It was looking like a lost cause and my savings were taking a hit.

Shortly after the conclusion of the 1985 season, Cornie and I bumped into George Strawbridge at Tampa Bay Downs. He showed no remorse for not warning us of his premonition that soccer had peaked and the team was doomed. Instead, he said, "Owning that team is like making a contribution to the American Red Cross." He was right. It was charity work, paying for a service that only a few used.

To add insult to injury, owning the team was not benefiting the Hall of Fame Inn as I'd hoped it would. I thought hordes of loyal Rowdies fans would frequent my establishment simply because I owned their team. No one cared. The sport's popularity was rapidly declining. With the expenses of the lease and the taxes and upkeep on the inn and golf course, I was barely earning enough money to pay the bills. I was breaking even on the airport lease while the Rowdies sucked my personal accounts dry.

It was time to break ties with the Rowdies. I desperately wanted to sell the team, but I had no takers. It had no fan base or league. Who would want to invest in a business like that? Just when I was about to announce that the team would be folded, I got an offer. Someone wanted to take over the team—my wife.

Cornie did not want to see the Tampa Bay Rowdies disappear into the history books. She felt they were too important to the community. Although the adult fan base had diminished, she believed the children in the community needed the Rowdies. Soccer might not have been a popular adult sport, but it was widely popular among children. She believed that if children had professional athletes from the sport they loved providing them with advice on topics such as avoiding drugs, alcohol, tobacco, cursing, violence, and so on, they might be more willing to listen.

By that time, our family had grown to four children, but Cornie and I were blessed to have help with our home life. When our third child, Alyda, was born in 1979, we put an ad in the paper for a live-in couple. Fortunately for us, a New Zealand couple, Trevor and Noreen, were looking for an opportunity to move to the states. They were grafted onto our family and stayed with us for 20 years. Trevor was especially important to our son Rick, born in 1982. In many ways, he was a surrogate grandfather and the two remained close until Trevor's death.

Cornie has always been active in the community and with our children's education, but having Trevor and Noreen keeping the household running freed her up in a way that she could use her gifts for opportunities like this one, to help all the children in our area.

Cornie wouldn't give me any money for the team, but she agreed to assume all debt and operational expenses if I sold it to her for zero dollars. I thought she was crazy, but I love her and have always supported her decisions. We signed the contracts, and in 1986 Cornie became the first woman to own a professional soccer team in the United States. She ran the team like a woman—and I mean that as a compliment. She treated everyone on the team like they were her children. Newspapers referred to her as "Team Mom." She sat next to the players on the bench, brought them dinner after practices, and dispensed advice to individuals whenever she felt they were going through tough personal times.

On top of Marsh's coaching duties, Cornie added the title of general manager of the Tampa Bay Rowdies. The team had a salary cap of $75,000 and she allowed Rodney to hire and fire players as he pleased, as long as he stayed under the cap. She did not want to step on his toes; she acknowledged she was not soccer savvy.

But she *was* business savvy.

She negotiated spots for the Rowdies in new soccer leagues: the American Indoor Soccer Association for one season, then the American Soccer League (ASL), and finally the American Professional Soccer League (APSL). She also operated soccer clinics featuring the Rowdies players for the local children. The games continued to draw just a few thousand fans a game, but merchandising was up from my few years as owner because the children continued to hound their parents for Rowdies shirts, hats, soccer balls, and so on. The money she earned from selling merchandise to the children was not the reason she offered the soccer clinics, though. She truly felt the children needed role models from the professional sports community, as proven by her children's ticket program, enabling children who purchased a season pass for $10 to buy individual game tickets for only a dollar.

But by 1993, despite Cornie's best efforts, as the team continued to lose money, she finally decided it was time to let the Rowdies go. She no longer had the time needed to run the team properly. No one wanted to buy the team, so in 1993, the Tampa Bay Rowdies officially folded.

It was a sad day for the Corbett family.

I don't look at our ownership of the Tampa Bay Rowdies as a failure though. True, the team folded under our watch and it did not have the effect on the Hall of Fame Inn I'd hoped that it would, but without the Rowdies the International Plaza might never have been completed. Ultimately, the Rowdies made me rich—not with cash, but in name recognition. As long as the Rowdies were playing soccer, the Corbett name was in the newspapers regularly. Whether it was good press or bad, it was press. We no longer needed the Fergusons to introduce us around town. All the most influential people knew who we were and had become our friends, friends who enabled my dream of the International Plaza to become a reality.

CHAPTER 16

Before I Could Be a Joe Kennedy, I Had to Be a Daniel Boone

One of the first people Chester Ferguson introduced me to in Tampa was Jim Warren, senior executive vice president of Tampa's First Florida Bank. Warren, through his bank, provided me with the loan to purchase the airport lease. With his well-cropped hair, three-piece pinstriped suits, and uncalloused white-collar hands, it was easy to mistake him for a boardroom warrior, the type of man who shivered at the thought of a weekend away from the comforts of home and modern conveniences. But beneath the suit, Warren was a bona fide adventurer, the type of man whose idea of a weekend getaway was being dropped off deep in the wilderness, not a man-made path in sight, with nothing more than his hands, fishing pole, knife, and survival skills at his disposal.

We were made of the same stuff, and during one of our first nonbusiness encounters, we tried to one-up each other with our out-doorsman stories. He frequently planned week-long outdoor adventures with other Tampa businessmen and in July 1979, shortly after we met, he invited me along. The excursion was a rafting trip down the Middle Fork Salmon River, otherwise known as "the river of no return," a 106-mile journey through Idaho's pristine and uninhabited wilderness. It was a well-earned nickname. Once your raft was plunged into the 400-plus-mile river and swept up by the current, the only way home was to finish the journey. The current was too strong to paddle against and the brush was without manmade paths—too thickly grown to hike through. And when the journey was done, the only way home was by air. Even Lewis and Clark, two of the greatest explorers in the history of this nation, deemed the Salmon River too dangerous to negotiate.

We wanted an adventure, yes, but we didn't want to die. None of us was experienced enough to control a regular raft on such a long and perilous journey, which took four days and five nights. We'd need a Guth raft, used primarily for dangerous white waters. The basic design of the raft, which is 20 feet long by 9 feet wide, is similar to that of a 10-man army raft, though considerably more comfortable. The tubing, a massive 40 inches, can carry 2,500–3,000 pounds. The raft is too large to paddle or row; the current moves it—and you. The raft is steered using long, thick oars called sweeps, and is so large that going through even the most dangerous white water can feel insignificant, like driving over a speed bump in a tank.

Whenever we broke for camp, we spent our time sightseeing, exploring, swimming, and trying to decipher the Native American carvings we discovered on mountainsides and fossilized trees throughout the wilderness. Fishing was tremendous and included various species of trout and salmon.

At night, with no radio, television, newspaper, or contact with the outside world, we sat around the fire on Cocktail Rock looking over our campsite which we named Resurrection City. And we talked about life. We talked about our businesses, our families, our dreams, our successes, and our failures. This particular wildlife trip was one of the most remarkable I'd ever taken. The sights were something I'll never forget. But what made the trip invaluable was the camaraderie that blossomed and grew each evening among us. It enabled me to get to know each of my fellow adventurers: Tom Shannon, former University of Florida quarterback; Jeff Wooley, owner of Superior Pontiac; Les Olsen, owner of Griffin Air Conditioning; Mike Annis, attorney; Tom McEwen, *Tampa Tribune* sports editor and columnist; and a handful of others.

When the trip began, most of my fellow travelers were strangers to me. By the end of the trip, they were my friends and continue to be friends today. Over the years, we've gone on countless adventures together to some of this country's most gorgeous wilderness destinations. Perhaps the most memorable was our July 1984 trip to Alaska, a trip that was almost my last.

Eight of us were on the Alaskan expedition: Warren, McEwen, Olsen, Annis, and me from the previous trip, plus Dick Beard, a Tampa high-rise developer; E.C. Smith, a teacher at Berkeley Prep; and Joe Taggart, a major Tampa developer and our neighbor. The six-day trip began in Anchorage, where we stayed in a tiny inn for a day until our propjet was ready to take us 200 miles southwest to a gravel landing strip on the northeast side of Lake Iliamna. With 24 hours to kill and no hunting or fishing near our inn in Anchorage, we went shopping. Numerous expeditions to various parts of Alaska began in Anchorage, so hunting and fishing stores were abundant. The store I wandered into was full of the latest hunting and fishing gadgets and equipment. With nothing better to do than spend money, my eyes were wide with wonder at everything.

I wanted all of it.

Fortunately, I have strong willpower when it comes to spending money. Truth is, I'm probably the cheapest person you'll ever meet. I was easily able to avoid any impulse buying, but there was one item I couldn't pass up—a pair of Goodyear rubber chest waders. I'd been informed that the waters we'd be fishing would be icy cold. I figured the chest waders were a practical purchase, but my friends tried to talk me out of it. They said chest waders would, in fact, put my life in danger. The current was fast and often knocked over fisherman. If I fell down into the water, the waders could easily and quickly fill with water, and I'd be helpless in the water's rush. I'd be swept into the Bristol Bay, then perhaps into the Bering Sea, where I'd surely be lost until a search team was able to drag my dead body to land. They cautioned me to wear the usual knee waders and not venture too far out into the water.

I wouldn't listen. I'd been fishing all my life, I was in great shape, and I had great balance from boxing and skiing. There was no way I'd be knocked down from a sturdy perch. And we were fishing salmon. The best way to catch salmon is to wade into the water as far as possible so you can place the lure on the nose of the salmon heading up river to spawn. Arrogant and self-assured, I purchased the waders, laughing to myself that I would become the week's fishing king because I was the only fisherman with the *cojones* to use the chest waders.

The following day we flew to Lake Iliamna, where we were shuttled to Kokhanok Lodge in the four-seat, single-engine Cessna floatplanes that became our exclusive transportation for the rest of the week. We spent nights at the lodge and flew to each day's fishing destination in the morning. The fishing spots were far from our lodge and involved dangerous terrain. Perhaps in our teenage years we would have tried to hike it, but we all have to admit at some point in our lives that we can no longer do what we once did. Planes were the practical way to get to our fishing holes.

The lodge sat on a hill between the Copper River and Dream Creek. Our water supply, a powerful 30-yard-wide waterfall, pounded outside the lodge. It was probably the purest water I'd ever tasted. The lodge consisted of three two-person bedrooms all connected to a center room used for card playing and old-fashioned storytelling around a stove. Another one-room cabin for two was located a few dozen yards away from the lodge. I got to share that cabin with Tom McEwen. We jokingly called it the Septic Suite because the lodge's tank was located directly behind it.

There was no running water and the stream water was too cold for bathing, so we had to create a makeshift hot bath. We built what locals called a maqii, and threw a tent over a couple of benches next to the stream, built a stove out of an old oil drum, and rigged a pipe to take the smoke out of the top of the tent. We piled river rocks around the stove and stoked a fire to heat them. When the hot rocks were splashed with the cold water, steam was released creating a steam bath in the tent that kept us warm enough to bathe in the cold water. It was like taking a hot steam and a cold bath at the same time. The steam pulled the poisons out of our pores and the cold water provided us with a shot of vitality. It was quite a rush. But I was the only one crazy enough to do a bungee leap into the frigid lake.

The fishing was also successful. Beard and Taggart caught the biggest fish, a 35-pound king salmon and a 30-pound king salmon, respectively. Warren caught the biggest rainbow trout, a 5-pounder, and Smith caught the largest red salmon, a 25-pounder. And I was, well, not the king I envisioned I'd become. I was the jester.

I caught a sockeye salmon and began to reel him in, but as I pulled back on the rod, I slipped and fell into the water. My chest waders filled up quickly with water, turning me into a sinking balloon, just as my companions had warned. It was impossible for me to swim. I was helpless against the current. Swept up, my body rushed downstream with the salmon. I thought I was a dead man. Luckily, Smith was a dozen or so yards downstream. He saw me darting toward him, leaped into the water, grabbed me around the neck, and wrestled me to shore.

Believe it or not, after I thanked him for saving my life, I went back to my fishing spot—full-body waders still on—and repeated the performance a few hours later. Once again, Smith saved my butt. Pulling me onto shore the second time, he looked me in the eye and said, "Enough of you. You're not allowed to fish anymore today." I did take the rest of the day off, and I was the butt of jokes for the remainder of the trip (and for years to come). But it was all good, old-fashioned ribbing among friends.

That's what those trips were all about—the friendships. You can't spend days in the wilderness, away from modern conveniences and distractions like radios or TVs, and not become close with everyone in the group. The fundamental character of human relationships comes out clearly in such settings—the good parts as well as the bad. Fortunately, nearly all of the circumstances in the dozens of my small-group excursions created positive bonds that became deeply rooted in long-term relationships. These men, whom I met as adults, became as close as long-held childhood friends. It was as if we were members of a secret club. Most of the people back home saw us as suit-wearing boardroom stiffs, but we knew the truth about one another. Deep down inside, we were all natural wild men, bonded together by the challenges and insanities of roughing it in untamed territory, like Tarzan. To this day, these men, with whom I've shared unique experiences and countless memories, remain among my closest friends in Tampa.

My fellow adventurers were also a who's who of the Greater Tampa Bay power structure at the time. I did not befriend them because of who they were socially, but I'd be lying if I didn't recognize how their friendships helped me with business deals over the years. We all wound up helping each other. That's how effective social systems work.

Successful communities and businesses derive their traction from the political realities of relationships among people. And it starts among small groups of like-minded people, grounded either in blood (family) or commonality of interests (such as business success). Personal knowledge and skill are important, but who you know does more than grease the wheels of success. It forms the tracks that help make success possible. Without colleagues and friends in positions of influence and leverage in public and private settings, big-time business deals are nearly impossible to pull off. If one of my outdoor compatriots could not directly help me with a business problem, he usually knew someone who could. Those friendships connected me to every corner of the community. And many of those people and the web of relationships created with them helped me move the International Plaza deal through hard, often treacherous times into success years later.

I also made connections with people in high places through civic endeavors, after being introduced to the idea by my friend Jay Wolfson. We met in the mid-1980s, when we both had children attending Independent Day School, and our friendship grew over the course of several years. Whenever we attended the same school event, we would gravitate toward each other. He was a fascinating man to talk to, with so many interests. A professor at University of South Florida and vice president of an academic health complex, Wolfson holds a doctorate in public health and graduate degrees in public health and history. He was a senior Fulbright scholar at the University of Tokyo Medical School, a faculty scholar to the Centers for Disease Control and Prevention, and a W.K. Kellogg Scholar in health-care finance. And after accomplishing all of that, he decided to earn a law degree.

Wolfson exercises vigorously and loves to ride motorcycles. He's a true renaissance man—and one of my closest friends and confidants. We often enjoy spending days ripping through the back roads of Tampa in our cars or quietly sitting by the lakes behind our respective homes, sipping drinks and talking. Because we both have so many interests and know each other and each other's families so well, we can talk for hours. There are few men on this planet whose opinions I respect more than Wolfson's. I often share personal and business issues with him, trusting that he will weigh everything before offering me advice, and knowing that he will always be the most discrete consigliere.

Years after I met him, he became something of a household name when he was appointed to serve as the special guardian ad litem for Terry Schiavo, reporting to the governor and courts on her behalf. Schiavo was the St. Petersburg woman who suffered brain damage due to cardiac arrest and lapsed into a persistent vegetative state. Her husband and parents spent years fighting in the courts and in the press over her legal guardianship. The parents wanted her to remain on life support, but her husband felt his wife was already deceased and wanted her off the support. Wolfson was caught in the middle of it all and did important work, universally recognized as unbiased and grounded firmly in good medicine and good law.

Despite everything with which he was involved, he still found time to give back to the community, speaking regularly on radio and television about important matters involving the health-care industry and serving for 12 years on the Tampa General Hospital Board. He continues to do research, write articles and books, and find ways to weave history, politics, science, medicine, and human nature comfortably into the many topics that capture his attention. Though even busier than I was, he found time to do things that didn't involve making himself wealthier.

I, on the other hand, dedicated my every waking moment to earning a profit. As our friendship grew, I sometimes felt guilty about my lack of community involvement. He never rubbed it in that he did so much for the community. He didn't need to. It was enough just being around him and hearing him talk in passing of the civic responsibilities he undertook.

Wolfson was not the only important friend of mine involved in the community. George Steinbrenner, for example, worked 25 hours a day and 8 days a week running the New York Yankees, yet still was able to give time to numerous charities. He even read Christmas stories to underprivileged kids every holiday season. Indeed, every one of my important friends found time to help themselves *and* the community, yet I had not played in both arenas.

In the late 1980s, I decided it was time for me to give back to the community. My first civic venture was joining the Tampa General Hospital Foundation Board of Trustees and later the Tampa General Hospital Board of Directors. I later served on the boards of directors for the Florida Council of Economic Education and the Hillsborough Education Foundation. I became active in the Tampa Chamber of Commerce, the Museum of Science and Industry, and the Boy Scouts of America. In the mid-1990s, I was instrumental in the campaign to get the Community Investment Tax (CIT) passed in Hillsborough County. I worked alongside then-Mayor Dick Greco and political activist George Levy to ensure that the county voters supported the tax in the voting booth. The CIT was a countywide halfpenny sales tax used to fund the police and firefighters, build new schools, and repair the county's crumbling infrastructure, as well as provide the Tampa Bay Buccaneers with a new stadium—

Raymond James Stadium. Without the tax, the Bucs would have left Tampa Bay, policemen and firefighters would have been understaffed, schools would have had to go on double session to accommodate all the students, and infrastructure such as county and city plumbing and roads and parks and recreation centers would have fallen into such disrepair that they may never have been able to be righted. I was beginning to realize how much value there was in giving time and energy and knowledge back to the community.

Few efforts were as personally gratifying as when I was appointed by Governor Jeb Bush to the Florida Fish and Wildlife Conservation Commission. Yes, as in *Republican* Jeb Bush. After I went to work for myself, I began to embrace more conservative ideals. I remained a registered Democrat for many years in loyalty to my father, but voted Republican for every president from 1972 on. I finally made it official in 1983 when then Tampa Mayor (later Florida Governor) Bob Martinez switched.

I was on the political radar in 2003, when Bush was seeking candidates for the Florida Fish and Wildlife Conservation Commission. Some of his confidantes recommended me and he selected me to be one of seven members to serve this exceptionally important and influential statewide board, which is charged with governing Florida's fish and wildlife resources.

Commissioners serve five-year terms, and it's highly unusual to serve longer. I managed to be reappointed by two more governors—Charlie Crist and Rick Scott—serving a total of 12 years, including two years as chairman.

I will never forget my first commission meeting. These gatherings are enormously controversial; they regularly draw people who are passionate about protecting wildlife, very often to the exclusion of everything else, including human safety. An important item on the agenda had to do with the problem of feral cats, specifically 10 million diseased, nonhousehold felines. The question was whether they should be trapped, neutered, and rereleased, or euthanized.

The commission members were escorted in by armed guards—wildlife officers as well as sheriff's deputies and police. Hundreds of people were there with posters and screaming various slogans that boiled down to *leave our little kittens alone*. It was like a circus and there was no room for common sense. The next item was manatees—a topic just as emotionally charged and political.

My service was not without controversy, as I firmly believe that overprotecting wildlife can create a weakness and imbalance in the natural flow of nature. And that view is not shared by the vocal special interest groups that attend those meetings. However, I did my best on that commission during the years I served and am proud to be credited with, among other things, helping to pass a constitutional amendment in 2008 that will help preserve the long-leaf pine and wiregrass habitat for quail, as well as launching the Florida Youth Conservation Network, which has the motto, "Creating the next generation that cares."

In spite of the challenges of civic service, I will remain forever grateful that I was given the opportunity, thanks to the inspiration of Jay Wolfson, who taught me how satisfying it is to give back to the community. It provided me ample opportunity to leave what I believe has been a more positive mark on the world.

My personal and political connections allowed me to join boards of prominent civic organizations and make contributions to their important work. If I had not had these opportunities and instead tried to work my way up and into the hierarchy of these organizations, by working at a soup kitchen, for example, or selling tickets to fundraisers, I can't say I would have been as involved. I know that I have a lot to offer, but most of my life I wasn't interested in or willing to do the grunt work in the trenches of organizations (except in the mail room at the Kennedy White House!). The foot soldiers—the people who do the detail work—are the unsung heroes of the civic world. They dedicate hours and years of sweat to the causes in which they so passionately believe and rarely get public recognition.

I believe both roles are important and both require sacrifice.

I admit that I got as much out of fulfilling my civic responsibility as I gave. The work introduced me to more people who could help me with my endeavors and it further pushed me into the realm of "major player in Tampa." I was no longer just a rich businessman. I had become an important and recognized part of making our community better. And that becomes a natural feedback loop, because people from all parts of society—from candidates for president of the United States to sales workers at the mall—are more willing to help those they know help others.

Further strengthening my friendships with Tampa's major players was Cornie's family's Pinckney Hill Plantation located in the Red Hills region of North Florida. It is a distinctive part of Cornie's family heritage and has been called one of the best-managed wild quail habitats existing today, worldwide. These 17,500 acres of rolling terrain abuts the Georgia state line and provides one of the highest-quality habitats for all fish and wildlife species endemic to the long-leaf pine and wiregrass ecosystems. The land, which has been in Cornie's family since the 1930s, is dotted with lakes and ponds, and is a working farm as well, producing cotton, soybeans, and peanuts. It's also a quintessential hunting area rich in quail, dove, deer, duck, turkey, rabbits, and squirrels. The family lodge sits high above Raysor Lake and has an in-house team of cooks and helpers, many of whom are third-generation employees of the plantation. It also has its own stable of horses, dog kennels, and marked trails for riding, hunting, or exploring. It is an outdoorsman's paradise and an exceptionally rare thing to have in a family. Pinckney Hill has played a very important part of my personal and business life.

In many ways, it has provided mini adventures, like those I shared with Jim Warren and other businessmen in the Tampa community, but with more refinement. I've regularly invited political and business dignitaries for weekend getaways at the plantation. This has included presidential candidates, governors, senators, mayors, developers, bankers, CEOs, CFOs, and others who were thrilled to be able to enjoy the natural beauty and the historical importance of the plantation. Most of these people had become friends and colleagues over the years, and the plantation helped to cement existing or blossoming relationships. Many of them worked with me on multiple business deals, and I worked with them on theirs. Indeed, these relationships directly and indirectly helped to turn some of the most challenging political and financial corners that made International Plaza possible.

17

Getting Down to the Business of Making a Dream

From the first day that I saw the airport property, I knew that it could be something fabulous and profitable. Its proximity to the airport and its location within one of America's fastest-growing cities screamed out to me. This, in spite of the many people who said I was crazy to have gotten the land in the first place. They laughed and said it was folly to imagine transforming acres of airport land into a profitable venture—especially when I didn't have a specific plan—*and* by law the land had to be used for purposes that supported the airport.

Fortunately, I had a handful of friends and family who wanted to help.

By 1980, I had grown close with Dick Greco, an icon of Tampa politics and its former mayor. He had become vice president for the DeBartolo Corporation, one of the largest mall developers in the United States at the time. Greco is one of the most colorful, sincere, and kind men I've ever met. Like Will Rogers, he has never met a man or woman he hasn't loved instantaneously and almost everyone loves him back. He greets everyone, both men and women, with a warm embrace and a kiss on the cheek. And his sincerity and genuineness are infectious. He's the type of man you can meet once, talk with for five minutes, not see him again for five years, and he'll still remember your name and everything about you. He has a way of making everybody feel like his best friend. It makes him a natural politician and one of the city's most popular mayors. But in addition to being a lovely person, he possesses hard-core management skills and he knows how to make the city and its systems—public and private—work.

He was mayor of Tampa initially from 1967 to 1974 and turned a city with a small-town feel into a thriving metropolis. He served again from 1995 to 2003. His major accomplishments included eliminating a century-old illegal gambling ring that had plagued the city, integrating City Hall and ending racial strife within it, and making the political process participatory, rather than an "old boys' club" system. Greco thrived on luring major corporations to relocate their operations and headquarters to Tampa. Though I met him early in his business career, he was already a star on the rise. Edward DeBartolo would send Greco to cities where he wanted to develop mall properties and operations. And Greco would always find a way to win over the hearts and minds of public officials and residents—even in places where his political history was not known. In seven years as mayor, Greco never had an initiative turned down by the city council and, while working for DeBartolo, he never had a development proposal turned down by a city.

Not only did Greco have contacts throughout every level of government, he also understood how to get developments approved. If you were doing any development work, he was a vital person to have in your corner—and he was firmly in mine. We had a lot in common. Our first loves were politics and development and we were both avid hunters. Greco is actually one of the best shots I've ever met. As a teenager, he was a national champion skeet shooter and that skill naturally translated to success in the hunting field. It was there that we met, on a quail hunt to be exact, through the hunting buddies I made in 1979.

Greco often visited me at the Hall of Fame Inn for a drink and good conversation. We would talk about my struggle to find a way to transform the airport property into a profitable venture. He suggested that his boss, Edward DeBartolo, might have a few good ideas. DeBartolo was as tough as they come. I once heard that he underwent a hernia operation in the morning and was back in the office by the early afternoon. According to the legend, when someone asked how he could work in so much pain, he replied that he would be in just as much pain in bed.

DeBartolo was born with no wealth, no assets, and succeeded with no help from anyone. His father died before he was born, leaving his mother to raise six children on her own. He was embarrassed by his modest upbringing and worked hard to hide his true identity and to convince his fellow Youngstown, Ohio, residents that he came from a financially stable family. To do so, he worked numerous odd jobs as a teenager so that he always had money in his pocket. He used the money he saved to put himself through college at the University of Notre Dame. He then launched a successful career in real estate and development.

His story resonated deeply with mine. DeBartolo was my life and business soul mate; we clicked from the start and he wanted to help me with my airport lease. He told me that he had chosen mall development because retail business ventures had the largest payoff in the long run. He said with a plot of land as large as mine, the only way to optimize every inch of it was with retail stores. He envisioned developing the largest high-end fashion mall in the state on my land. Talk about big dreams!

I didn't know the first thing about retail stores or malls, but we shared countless hours in discussion and he allowed me to pick his brain. He also instructed me, and I asked about everything from zoning issues to how to lure an anchor store such as Macy's or Sears to a retail site. I never promised him I would go the retail route; nor did I promise I would partner with him if I did. He helped me anyway. By the time I was done asking him questions, I felt as though I'd graduated with a degree in mall development. Because of his tutelage, I realized the limitless financial potential a mall could have.

But there was one problem with all the information; it appeared to be useless. I worked on the idea for two years but couldn't come up with a way to make a mall fit under the "airport use" guideline. In 1982, I identified another route toward monetizing the land. The Tampa International Airport's executive director, George Bean, continued to regularly visit the inn's restaurant for breakfast. It had been his idea to rebrand the old motel the Hall of Fame Inn. It seemed like a grand idea at the time, but it was not panning out the way I'd hoped it would. Because I was not turning a large profit, I couldn't afford the necessary upkeep on the rooms. They were beginning to become dilapidated. The Hall of Fame Inn became a joke in Tampa, renamed by the press and others as the "Hall of Shame Inn."

Sometime early in 1982, I told Bean that I was disappointed with the direction the inn was taking. "George, I got this lady all dressed up," I told him. "I got her on the dance floor and I thought she would be so attractive that everyone would want to dance with her.

Instead she got drunk, stumbled, and fell." He laughed at my analogy, but I didn't crack a smile. I was serious and I was becoming desperate. I needed to figure out a way to make that land profitable. When he sensed my anxiety, he told me he would help me come up with a development plan. Just as airport officials once thought that a golf course could bring business to the airport, Bean thought a new, major development catering to travelers might help the airport grow. It was in his best interests to see me succeed.

The type of clientele that helps an airport grow fast and large is international business travelers. They travel the most and spend the most money. We decided that I would provide for such travelers on my property, offering a development catering to the "airport use clause."

I explored every concept imaginable for airport-related uses and even asked Bean to accompany me to a "think tank" at the Harvard University Graduate School of Design. He welcomed a trip back to his native Massachusetts, near his old home of Worcester. A friend of mine, a visiting professor of architecture, introduced the idea to a group of graduate students who made it their class project. They pitched us on a variety of concepts, such as trade centers, a mixed-use hotel, and even a space shuttle launching facility similar to the Kennedy Space Center on the east coast of Florida. Bean and I were intrigued by the trade center and hotel concepts.

I could rent office space to international corporations and their clients and employees could fly into Tampa, meet at the international corporation's office, attend a meeting or conference hosted by the corporation, and stay at a hotel, all within a few minutes' drive of the airport. It was brilliant! Executed correctly, the plaza could become an international business epicenter and help the airport grow.

But after further study and analysis, I realized that such a project was still too small. It would not allow me to use all of my land. I needed to make money off every inch of the land I was paying for if that lease was going to be worth it. That's where DeBartolo's idea finally blossomed. I suggested to Bean that I develop the hotel, offices, and conference center, as well as a retail and restaurant component. I could sell the airport on DeBartolo's idea because the retail and restaurant component would provide the business travelers and those who worked in the trade center a place to relax and shop. Thus, the plan fit under the "airport use" guideline, making the airport happy. The mall would be open to the general public, earning me the type of money I needed to make the venture worthwhile—and making me *very* happy. Bean loved my plan and told me he would help me sell it to the Aviation Authority. That's how the International Plaza's vision was born.

For the project to break ground, the Hillsborough County Aviation Authority first had to rezone the area to fit such a large development and provide me with an extended lease with more affordable rent. The extended lease was just as important as the more affordable rent. When a lease like that expires, the public has the opportunity to bid on leasehold rights. Under the original lease I held, if I were to be outbid at the end of the relatively short lease period, everything I built could be razed or the new lease owner could charge me extraordinary rent to continue to use the property. That could essentially push me out of the very project I had designed and developed—kind of like what happened to Steve Jobs after he built Apple into a successful company and was fired by its board. (As we know, he was brought back several years later to build it into an even more successful venture.)

In my case, getting a project the size and complexity of International Plaza off the ground would take years, and unless I could reduce the lease payments on what was essentially unusable land producing no income during the developmental period, I couldn't afford to pursue the design and development of the income-producing asset in the first place. I needed to be able to convince the airport authority that the lease needed to be reformed in two ways: (1) extend it for a period long enough to make it worth building and holding, and to protect me from somebody taking the lease over too soon; or (2) lower the rent I was paying so that I could afford to develop it.

I discussed the ideas with my good friend and Florida attorney Stella Thayer, along with Chip Davidson, a bright young real estate entrepreneur from Atlanta, and told them to get right to work on the modifications to the lease.

Davidson and I had become acquainted during the Black Island deal. He was still in Harvard Business School and was working with Bob Troutman. He later worked with Gerald Hines, one of the largest real estate developers in the United States. I saw Davidson's potential and stayed close with him, often asking his advice on business deals I had pending.

As most businessmen will tell you, the easiest way to stay financially secure is to hold on to as much of your money as you can. Whether that means using somebody else's money to make investments, or finding ways not to have to pay the government money that you've earned, the principle is the same.

My father had moved down to Tampa a year or so earlier to retire but quickly got caught up in my business venture. He too saw its potential. As a retired attorney, he still knew the law inside and out. I would often consult with him on issues I faced—zoning, leases, dealing with the government, and so on—and he invariably provided me with valuable advice. He also grew close to George Bean. My father would visit the Hall of Fame Inn's restaurant each morning, and whenever Bean was there, the two would sit together, relax with a cup of coffee, and talk about life. Not only was my father an experienced attorney, he was an attorney whom the Airport Authority trusted. My father took the lead on legal matters.

And he made it happen.

On November 15, 1982, the Hillsborough Aviation Authority rezoned the land to fit the vision of the International Plaza and extended my lease from 20 to 75 years. It was a sweet accomplishment. I couldn't help recalling comments from the people told me it was impossible to get the property rezoned. They said the businesses allowed on the property would never turn the type of profit needed to make the lease profitable. And they called me an idiot! But I believed in my vision and myself.

Once I succeeded in getting the land rezoned and getting a 75-year lease, the lease became a coveted asset. For a few months following the contract's signing, I was inundated with calls from developers from around the globe who wanted to purchase the lease from me. The standard offer was $75 million. I refused. I had sunk about $8 million into the enterprise by that point and selling it for such a profit would have been the safe thing to do. But since when had I ever played it safe? I wanted to develop the land and complete what I set out to do.

By 1985, I was wondering if I should have sold the lease when I had the chance. The project had been stalled for three years at that point. I had won rezoning, but I had a variety of other issues and each of them involved all levels of government. For instance, I needed roadways vacated around the property. I also needed new roads built on it and leading into it. Different roadways fell under different levels of government (city, county, or state). I also needed to purchase or have adjoining tracts rezoned to fit the development's needs. I could not allow other developers to dictate what went up around me. This meant that I had to deal with the various property owners, but, like the roads, different tracts fell under the jurisdiction of different levels of government. I needed to resolve sewage problems and other public utility issues. The work was like building a city from scratch on the borders of four separate states. I was in permit and infrastructure hell, with no end in sight. Compounding the problems, 1985 was the year I became sole owner of the Rowdies. I was head of two business ventures—both of which were losing money.

To make the dream of the International Plaza economically feasible, I needed to again renegotiate my rent and extend my lease. I couldn't afford to waste 20 years of my lease without earning a penny. I needed the time it was taking me to build the plaza added back on to my lease.

The Aviation Authority was on my side. They wanted the International Plaza. They extended my lease another 23 years for a total of 95 years, through the year 2080, and included a $1.4 million discount on rent in the immediate future and a rent increase pyramid that raised the land rent by only 5% every 10 years. I then turned to my powerful friends throughout the state and asked them to help in lobbying the various government entities on my behalf. Having influential friends in leadership certainly does help, and most of my permit and infrastructure problems were addressed by the end of 1985.

By 1986, however, despite the generous deal, I had more trouble—financial trouble. I was around $13 million in debt, but it appeared help was on the way. A British company was interested in building a trade center on the property. They were willing to pay me up to $9 million for the rights to build and I was ready to jump on the deal but after aggressive negotiations with my attorneys, they decided not to play.

I was in trouble. I had little income and a lot of money going out, forcing me to borrow heavily against my ground lease on the airport property. Shortly after the British deal fell through, Cornie joined with me and signed a personal guarantee for a new $13.5 million consolidated note payable to Florida Federal Savings. In 1987, I demolished the inn and golf course. The numbers were diminishing on both and they were beginning to cost me money to run. I would rather have nothing on the land than another two financial drains.

Despite my debt, I pushed on with the project. In 1989, I began looking for a partner on the retail component. Malls are a collection of stores, restaurants, and bars and each has its own development and management team. A mall developer must oversee the construction of the mall facility plus all the retail, restaurant, and bar developers. One needs to be focused to handle such a task. I could not oversee a development the size of the International Plaza and manage the development of a mall. I knew I needed to find an experienced mall developer with whom to partner.

DeBartolo seemed like the logical choice. We were friends, the retail component of the plaza was his idea, and he was one of the most successful mall developers in the United States. He was also offering me major cash up front and equal ownership as partners in mall. One thing I've learned from years of business, however, is not to partner with anyone simply out of friendship. Business and friendship must be separate. It's more important to find a good deal than to appease a friend. It takes a certain ruthlessness to succeed in the business deal, a ruthlessness I had to put on full display to get the best possible deal from a developer.

I also needed leverage. Leverage in the mall industry means getting a top retail store to anchor your development. When a mall signs an anchor like Sears or Macy's, other small to mid-range retailers follow because they know the large department stores get such high traffic that the spillover alone can sustain them. Banks are aware of this correlation, so signing a large retail store to anchor a mall also means it's easier to get financing for the mall's development. Mall developers are obviously aware of this, so if I could sign an anchor on my own I would be able to pick the developer I wanted for a partner. They all would want to be associated with a mall that would have an easier time finding bank financing.

Unfortunately for me, there was another project eerily similar to mine that was ready to steal all of my leverage—a project that threatened the very existence of International Plaza. The development was called the Tampasphere. It was planned about a mile away from my site, north of I-275, and was going to include four office towers connected by a mall and a hotel. The project was announced in 1983 but had faced numerous problems since then and had not yet broken ground. Partnership squabbles, financing, and zoning issues had held up the project. In the late 1980s, I received news from a friend that the Tampasphere was close to a major breakthrough. It was about to sign a big-time anchor tenant—Macy's.

Macy's, at the time, was one of the premier mall stores in the nation. If Tampasphere could sign Macy's, it would be able to find the financial partners it needed to move forward. If Tampasphere became a reality before International Plaza, I would be sunk. I'd be left with a long lease on empty property, no revenue to pay bills, and little of interest to entice investors. A few blocks from the Tampasphere's planned location, however, was Tampa's infamous Dale Mabry Boulevard plot of land, adorned with strip clubs. Another few blocks away was a city sanitation spot, and yet another few blocks away was a holding pen for county convicts. I had my ammunition. I drove through the strip club area one night with my camera and snapped photos when shifts were changing, which enabled me to capture photos of dozens of scantily clad women walking in and out of each club. I then took photos of the sanitation spot in mid-afternoon as the sun roasted and rotted the garbage. Finally, I photographed the holding pen while inmates were being delivered. All of my photography skills from high school were put to good use and served me very well.

I then snapped photos of my property, framing it in the best possible light, showing off the airport and only the surrounding businesses that enhanced the area. A few days later, armed with my photos, I was on a plane to New York to meet with a Macy's real estate officials. I showed him my photos of the Tampasphere's surrounding area and the photos of the International Plaza's surrounding area and said, "Which area do you think the ladies who shop at Macy's will want to frequent?" I gave him my business card and told him to think it over. The entire meeting lasted only a few minutes, but it was all I needed.

A few days later I received a call from one of the top mall developers in the nation, Taubman Centers. Bobby Taubman told me Macy's was considering pulling out of Tampasphere and moving into the International Plaza, instead. I had not even broken ground yet, and I was already winning the war against my closest competition. The Tampasphere, by the way, was a joint partnership between Tampa development mogul and political king maker, Al Austin and my old friend, NFL owner Hugh Culverhouse. It was ruthless, yes, but they would have done the same to me.

Once word got out that I had Macy's, I didn't have to call big mall developers and beg them for a good deal. They were all calling me. Macy's all but guaranteed the mall would be successful and that the mall developer could receive financing for his end of the project. DeBartolo made me a sweet offer—millions of dollars up front plus an equal ownership percentage of the mall. Several national mall developers offered me less than DeBartolo and it seemed that the DeBartolo deal would end up being the best. We were ready to execute the contract, until we learned that DeBartolo was experiencing significant financial difficulties with his lenders. Taubman then came to the table and offered me a similar deal, but also added commitments with more upscale retail chains, including Lord & Taylor, Neiman Marcus, and Saks Fifth Avenue. If I went with them, the International Plaza's mall would be the most upscale shopping destination in the state.

I went with Taubman. DeBartolo understood. We remained friends until the day he died, and Greco remains one of my closest friends to this day.

But trouble arrived in 1992 when Macy's filed for bankruptcy and stopped all expansion. Taubman said the only other acceptable national anchor tenant that would make the deal work was Nordstrom. The trouble with that plan was that Nordstrom was just beginning to branch out to the east and already had commitments in Connecticut; Washington, DC; and Atlanta. They wouldn't even consider a Florida location for another seven years.

Then, of course, the situation got worse.

18

CHAPTER

Who Shops at Malls, Anyway?

In 1990, my lender, Florida Federal, went under. The federal government's savings and loan cleanup agency, the Resolution Trust Corporation (RTC), then sued me the following year for defaulting on a balloon payment in September of 1990. The RTC took over the loan and filed a foreclosure lien against the leaseholder. I was in trouble. In May 1992, I asked to buy back the $13.5 million note from the RTC at a discounted rate. The request was refused. If the loan had to be eaten, the burden would fall on taxpayers. I understood their decision and would have paid the full amount had I been able. Unfortunately, I was not.

This put me in a tight spot. The RTC was fair, even though it had a lawsuit against me. It did not require me to make ridiculously overpriced monthly loan payments, nor did it jack up the interest to be spiteful. It allowed me to make reasonable payments with a reasonable interest rate. However, until I was up to date, a private credit bureau could have bought the loan and the RTC could have leveraged any interest rate it wished and at any monthly payment amount. Or even worse, it could have sold my lease.

Luckily for me, because of the size of the loan and because of how complicated it is to build on federal airport property, no one bought it. Luckily for me, I was the only one stupid enough to want to build there. Then my family and friends bailed me out yet again. Thayer organized a firm called CHAR, Inc., and named Cornie's relatives to the board. CHAR then bought the loan and sold it back to me for $5.4 million, a number I could handle.

Finally, it seemed that the International Plaza was ready to move ahead. In May 1994, Taubman and I completed our partnership contract. A month later, in June 1994, Macy's signed a letter of intent to be part of the mall.

But soon after that, more trouble arrived. It seemed as if it would never end.

Al Austin, whose Tampasphere I screwed out of its Macy's deal, came looking for revenge. His project had collapsed. Stealing Macy's was not the sole reason it failed, but it was a major one. Austin is one of Tampa's top developers. He created the Westshore District when he erected the aptly named Austin Center, a community of hotels and business centers on 17 acres of land on Westshore Boulevard. As his center grew, so did the community around it, becoming the major metropolitan business and retail area it is today. He was also one of the top Republican leaders in the state of Florida. Austin's support meant dollars and votes. He personally donateded hundreds of thousands of dollars to the Republican Party and solicited millions. Austin was a moving force behind the election of Connie Mack to the US Senate. And his heart was as big as his wallet. He helped to develop Tampa Preparatory School. He secured the city and state funding needed to rehabilitate the University of Tampa minarets and donated countless amounts of money to countless charities. Not only was he well connected; his philanthropy and big heart made him well loved. He had the type of power that could squash most men and I was next on his hit list.

I was not intimidated. In the short time I'd been in Tampa, I had accumulated a number of powerful friends of my own—many of whom Austin would normally have looked to for support in such a situation. Because these friends were mutual, they stayed out of the business squabble. Ultimately, the powerful allies I acquired through the Rowdies, hunting trips, and civic work prevented Austin from ruining me.

When he realized that we had too many friends in common, he tried attacking me via the press. He began leaking false information to reporters throughout the state, claiming that I had gotten a sweetheart deal on my lease because I paid off city officials. For a month, reporters called me day and night, screaming questions to me about bribes and special arrangements. I answered every question that came my way. I had friends who worked for the daily newspapers and probably could have countered the attacks with positive press, but I didn't feel I had to go that route. I had done nothing illegal; I had nothing to hide.

A few articles accused me of various things, but nothing ever came of the mud-slinging. If anything in the articles had been true, I would have been arrested. Federal investigators never even opened a case on me. I wasn't guilty of any crimes.

But I was not on safe ground yet.

Come 1995, the International Plaza still had not materialized. The stall resulted from Tampa having become saturated with shopping destinations in those years and many of the malls and outlet stores were struggling financially because of it. The Floriland Mall, once a flourishing marketplace near Busch Boulevard, had fallen on such hard times that it had to be converted into a flea market. Sunshine Mall in Clearwater lost all of its department store anchors. And two other malls—Pinellas Square Mall in Pinellas Park and East Lake Square Mall in Tampa—were struggling with occupancy rates in the 60% range. Both were forced to recast themselves as "community centers," marketplaces for local and small regional stores. Crystal River Mall in Citrus County, which opened in 1990, had also been unable to keep its occupancy rate at over 60%.

Another powerful force undermining the value and success of traditional malls was the rapid growth and development of Walmart, Target, Circuit City, and other such superstores opening throughout the area and taking foot traffic away from the malls.

Because of the besieged mall scene, I was struggling to get the bank financing we needed—about $150 million for the entire plaza. Taubman would cover part of this total, but even he was having trouble getting a loan for the mall. Despite Macy's signing of a letter of intent with us, no bank saw a mall as a sound financial investment.

Not all malls were struggling. A few—Tyrone Square Mall in St. Petersburg, Westshore Plaza in Tampa, and Countryside Mall in Clearwater—continued to thrive. These malls actually had a waiting list of retailers trying to get in. They were succeeding because they were located in better areas. This list of successful malls was also a setback for me. Westshore Plaza was located only a few miles away from my property. If banks were already weary of mall financing, mine being located near a mall that had become a financial giant made them even more skeptical. Banks had a hard time believing I could compete with Westshore Plaza.

If I was going to compete, I needed to lower my annual land carrying cost. I needed to pay the Aviation Authority lower rent. My rent minimum was $700,000 a year, which sounds cheap for such a large parcel of land until you consider that I was not making a nickel off the land. The $700,000 was an annual cash loss of $700,000. Also blocking my ability to earn money off the land were the numerous and strict regulations the airport placed on the property. It took me nearly two decades to get the property development-ready. After all those years of development hell the airport's guidelines put me through, I deserved the break.

I asked that the minimum payment be dropped and for my rent that year to be reduced to $200,000. Airport officials knew my request was fair, but they were leery of such a deal. A few years earlier, the US Transportation Department auditors had threatened to yank the airport's federal funds because it was leasing federal land to me for what they considered to be below-market value. The Transportation Department claimed my lease was costing the airport millions of dollars in rent it could have been collecting from me. Nothing ever came of the threat because I *was* paying fair market value. Nonetheless, airport officials said that surely the US Transportation Department would revisit the threat if I were afforded lower rent without getting an appraisal of the land's value.

I commissioned Charles L. Knight to appraise the property. His appraisal stated that it was worth $2,925,000, or about $18,750 an acre. Those numbers indicated that my rent was too high. On February 1, 1996, Airport Authority voted to slash my rent to my requested number.

Some sectors of the community were outraged by this news. The media again wrote that I was bribing public officials. They wondered how it was legal for me to hire the appraiser rather than the airport, claiming it to be legal bribery. And I was accused of having two of my friends—Dave Mechanik, a zoning lawyer, and Dick Beard III, my old hunting and fishing buddy and a well-known developer— influence Knight's decision. I was not worried. They were baseless accusations.

I did not bribe anyone. It's true that I had friends on the authority, such as Greco (who once again became mayor in 1995) and Thayer. Thayer, however, abstained from the vote and Greco voted for what he thought was best for the community, not his friend. Considering I turned my back on his former boss, would he have broken the law to do me a favor? More important, Greco was not the type of man to break the law.

What's more, it's normal for a lease owner to pay for the appraisal and Knight would never allow my paying his bill to influence his decision. Indeed, Charles Knight was one of Tampa's most-respected community leaders and to accuse him of such a crime was offensive. Mechanik and Beard did provide Knight with information on the land, but all the data they provided him were accurate. The facts showed that the land was of little value because of all the zoning problems that came with it.

As I suspected, once I could offer lower rent, the tenants began lining up. In 1998, construction finally began. Phase 1 was the construction of an office building. The real estate agent representing the developer of the building was a fishing and hunting buddy, Joe Taggart. That same year, Taubman signed a number of tenants to the mall, enabling us to acquire the necessary bank loans to begin planning construction.

Local newspapers continued to slam me. At one point, the *St. Petersburg Times* wrote that I would have shortchanged the public out of $220 million by the time my lease was up in 2080. Total nonsense. The paper was judging the land by what its value would be when the plaza was complete. That's not how land value is determined. It's determined by its worth before the development breaks ground. An appraiser cannot speculate on what the land might be worth if the planned development becomes a success.

I was granted low rent because I took an enormous risk by purchasing a long-term lease on property fraught with zoning issues. I worked hard to make a project that most people deemed idiotic successful and I was reaping the rewards. That is the beauty of this country. Hard work, determination, and intelligence are rewarded.

In late 1999, the International Plaza's first office building opened and construction was nearly complete on the second. It should have been a time of great joy for me. It was instead a time of great stress. Also in late 1999, the inspector general of the US Department of Transportation recommended that the Federal Aviation Authority withhold all funds from the airport until the Aviation Authority amended the lease to provide for fair-market value. I pushed forward. I had done nothing illegal and knew that I would be vindicated when all was said and done.

I was right. In July 2000, the Federal Aviation Authority announced that after an intense investigation it determined that my deal was fair and handled properly.

Regardless of the decision, the bad press was starting to get to me. In a show of good faith, when the Hillsborough County Aviation Authority asked me to amend my lease at a higher rent, I agreed. I could have fought the decision and won, but paying more money was the easier thing to do. I just wanted to avoid any more battles.

Around that time, my old friend Jim Fusco swept into town and tried convincing me to purchase the land across the street from the plaza as well. He said he could help me find other financing and I would own that entire portion of Tampa. I turned him down. I could have easily taken a risk and acquired more land but my new business advisor, Dick Beard, was overly cautious and advised me to decline. Fusco reminded me of the old Dick Corbett—a risk taker. Fusco's vision was correct: once the plaza was completed that land's value skyrocketed.

Finally, in September 2001, after 22 years in the making, the entire International Plaza was almost done—the office space, the conference centers, the hotel, and the cornerstone of it all, the 1.26-million-square-foot indoor/outdoor mall boasting 200 stores and restaurants. This was my Merchandise Mart, my Joe Kennedy moment.

CHAPTER 19

A Day in the Limelight Becomes a Day of Darkness

For more than two decades, I pulled every string I could and spent all of my energy making International Plaza a reality. The result was the ultimate reflection of what I wanted it to become. And I wanted to have one hell of a party to show off the business accomplishment of a lifetime. The list of special invitees was literally the who's who of the community and the state and included my dearest friends from all over the country—people who had been on my journey with me for decades. I contracted to have more than $100,000 in food prepared. I would serve only the back-shelf, high-quality scotches, vodkas, and other liquors. I had friends, family, and work colleagues—everyone who stood by me throughout the long process—flown in for the occasion. I arranged for my old friend Jim Fowler, host of Mutual of Omaha's *Wild Kingdom*, to perform. We expected thousands of people to flood the mall moments after we cut the ribbon.

I had a fabulous speech planned, thanking everyone who made that day possible, specifically my father, who had passed away in 1996 and never got to share the experience with me. It was going to be *my* moment in the sun and the people closest to me knew that and supported it.

Three days before the formal mall opening, I sat in my living room and reviewed my speech as a handful of friends who were in town for the celebration sat glued to my television. My eyes were on my handwritten notes, and my inner voice was speaking the words. I was oblivious to the world around me. There was nothing else that could possibly be more important.

171

Until one of my friends said, "Dick, take a look at this. Someone just flew a plane into the World Trade Center!" Suddenly, I was snapped out of my trance, as if I had been kicked in the head.

It was September 11, 2001, and one of the saddest days in the history of our nation. I sat stunned and glued to the television, like the rest of the country, shocked and dazed by the impossibility. For the next 24 hours all I did was watch the news coverage of the tragedy and sit by the phone, calling and waiting for all of my family and friends in New York to return calls and tell me they were all right.

Incredibly, the night of September 11, 2001, was to be my personal party to celebrate all that I achieved. The greatest party I had ever planned, had to be canceled. I donated $100,000 in food to charity and canceled all the pomp and circumstance. How could I celebrate my life when so many people had lost theirs, and when the nation had been turned upside down? My ego told me to damn the torpedoes and hold the party. My heart and my head told me that could not happen. The tragedy and sorrow of September 11th stole the joy of my success from my heart.

Instead, on September 14, 2001, we opened the mall to little fanfare. We made the decision to go with a simple ribbon-cutting ceremony rather than a lavish party. Shipping delays caused by the disaster and airport shutdowns meant that more than a dozen stores could not even open that day, anyway.

Other circumstances added to the somber mood:

1. Because we were located next to the airport and because Tampa's MacDill Air Force Base is home to the US military's Central Command, the mall was surrounded by military sharpshooters. Nobody knew if there was going to be another "event," and there was genuine concern that the mall could become a target because of its Tampa location and because it was a great new symbol of American commerce.

2. On September 14, the skies opened up and drenched Tampa with a torrential, blinding rain that made driving dangerous.

3. We opened the ceremony with a prayer and the pledge of allegiance. That had always been the plan, but because of the attacks a few days earlier, these two customs carried a more powerful meaning than anybody could have imagined.

I remember looking around as the few dozen people said the pledge, and there wasn't a dry eye in the group. That pledge of allegiance took on a new and profoundly emotional force for my few close friends and family gathered. The kind of struggle that my Erie Canal great-grandparents had experienced—as well as their goal of creating self-sufficiency in the country through hard work and individualism—was at once being realized with the opening of the mall and yet threatened by the cowardly attacks on innocent people in New York; Washington, DC; and Pennsylvania. In one way, I felt a personal call to arms that day, because in my gut and in my bones, my family on both sides had been part of making this nation great. So we quietly celebrated the nation that provides its citizens with opportunities that allow them to fulfill their dreams—mine being the International Plaza—as we stood in the rain, cried, saluted the flag, and faced what we all knew was going to be a brave new world.

To this day, I still feel an emptiness—a huge missing piece—about the way things unfolded. Yes, I was robbed of my moment. Yes, my ego was slammed by not being able to celebrate the joy of completing my hard-fought battle to build the mall. And yes, I knew then and know now how selfish that is, especially in the face of the horrific disaster that changed so much for all of us. But it bugs me to this day, and it's hard to shake. I'd be dishonest if I didn't admit my disappointment.

But all of us are egocentric. It's part of being human and having expectations. And when those expectations aren't met, we feel hurt—indeed, cheated. I sure did. I was also saddened that my dad was not able to see the final product, though he knew I had "done good." I always fantasized that Dad would tip his hat to me, the way Jack Kennedy's dad did to him in front of the White House on Inauguration Day. And the unspoken sadness is that I never felt that I had made my mother proud, either. I was, for years, too bitter about her tragic life and death to think about doing so. All of those feelings were wrapped up in the mall opening. It was a bittersweet time.

CHAPTER 20

I Built Myself into Our Home

When my family and I moved to Tampa, I had no plan to build a plaza. Remember, I had made my bag of money, had "retired," and my plan was to grow the family with Cornie and settle into our new home. We originally moved into a north Tampa house in Carrollwood located on the seventh hole of a golf course. It was a gorgeous house and Cornie has always been an avid golfer, so to the objective eye, it was the perfect home for us. But I was never comfortable in it. I didn't feel it was mine or for me; it was temporary.

I am a developer. I developed our home in New York City and could never be comfortable living in a house I had no part in building. A home is built with more than bricks, mortar, wood, and nails. A big part of a real home is the souls and sweat and visions of those who design it and put it together. Every nail that's hammered, every wire that's spliced, every pipe laid, every splinter sanded has running through it a piece of every person who had a hand in that part of the construction. I could never be content in a home made up of the pieces of other souls, when not one piece came from me.

My part in the development of our carriage home in New York began and ended with the vision. I told the construction crew what I wanted and they turned my vision into reality. It had a piece of my soul in it. But I wanted my next home to have many pieces of me in it. My intention in Tampa was to participate both in the design and the hands-on construction of a home, from foundation through topping off.

In 1982, I found a piece of land that was perfect for the family home I wanted to build. I purchased an acre and a half of prime dirt in the gated, north Tampa country-club community of Avila. A gorgeous and challenging golf course is just behind my backyard, bordered by a 30-acre pond that attracts numerous birds and captures the reflection of both sunrise and sunset every day while perfectly mirroring rows of trees next to the shoreline.

We engaged Gerry Curts, a local architect, and Cornie worked on all of the details with him. My dream became a two-story, 15,000-square-foot home, complete with full-length pool, hot tub, billiards room, offices, guest quarters, and seven bedrooms. Once it was designed, I hired a general contractor and gave him two orders:

1. I wanted the home completed within one year, and
2. I wanted to work on the home's construction and not have anyone but him and the general foreman know I was the owner.

I didn't want preferential treatment. I wanted to experience what it was like to work my fingers to the bone every day as a grunt worker on my own home. If the other workers knew who I was, they would give me the easy jobs to do and kiss my ass. I wanted to actually build the home, not just pretend that I was building it.

Plus, I did not have much else to do. At that time, the International Plaza wasn't even conceived. I was a minority owner of the Rowdies and the airport property I owned was housed in a run-down, old airport inn on a golf course, on a plot of land that could not be rezoned. I was bored—a state in which I rarely found myself. Helping to construct my own home as an undercover worker was something I couldn't have imagined doing before or since. But this was a perfect hiatus in my life, and I filled it with a labor of love. Today, there are reality shows based on such things. I did it just for kicks.

The general foreman told the subcontractors that I was a day laborer who was skilled in a variety of trades and who would be hired when I was needed. Over the next year, the foreman allowed me to be a part of every crew that was assembling my home. I helped cut and lay the tiles for the floors. I helped install the plumbing and build my bathrooms. I worked with the roofers and the electricians. I assisted the air-conditioning team. I plastered ceilings and installed cabinets. I planted the trees and bushes. I did it all. It was one of the most gratifying experiences of my life. When I walk through my home today, I know I had a hand in building every inch of it.

Everything I look at has a story and a memory attached. Everything has a piece of me in it, a piece of my soul.

The work was also one of the most humbling experiences of my life. Although the crewmembers had no reason to doubt that I was a subcontractor and a day laborer, they realized on day one that the general foreman must have lied when he claimed I was skilled. I possessed little construction ability. While plastering the ceiling, pieces continually fell on my head. I couldn't cut tiles straight, and I didn't even know how to hold cabinets against the wall so that another worker could screw them in. My incompetence constantly aggravated my fellow workers, to the point where each crew's foremen argued over who had to use me that day. Even if a crew needed a worker, the foreman of that crew would sulk when he learned I'd be working for him. When I wasn't holding things up, I was screwing them up.

I was tempted on some days to save face and spill the beans, explain to everyone that the reason I was so inept was because I was not a real construction worker, that I was actually the signature on the big checks. But I was too proud to say anything. I was once a blue-collar guy back in Rochester. That was part of my heritage, and I rationalized that I was returning to my roots. I was actually embarrassed that I had grown so soft and so useless over the years; dedicating myself to a white-collar life had cost me my blue-collar roots. When I was a kid, I was capable of learning and doing anything, especially physical things. But as part of the house-building team, I felt incompetent, which only made me try even harder. I was determined to rediscover my groove as a blue-collar man again and *earn* the respect of the other guys on the construction site. I was not going to simply buy or command respect by announcing that I was their boss.

Though I never became the most-skilled worker on the team, I actually became fairly competent. By the end of the year, I was no longer a detriment to whomever I was assigned. I was able to provide valuable help. I grew close to many of the guys on the crew. Each Friday night I would hit the local bars with them, slamming back a few beers and talking about that week's work and life in general. I never let on who I really was. Even when Cornie would visit the construction site to see how things were going, I pretended that I didn't know her and she pretended she didn't know me. The other workers would all perk up a bit when she arrived, making sure to get the word out to look extra busy—not that they weren't working hard the rest of the time, but they all seemed sensitive to displaying a particularly good image when the owner was around. It was a matter of pride. And somehow, they never suspected anything. I guess with my crooked nose and broken fingers, I fit right in.

When the home was finally finished, I told everybody the truth. There was surprise, laughter and, I think, a degree of respect. Many admitted that in the early weeks, they could not figure out why the general foreman kept bringing me back when all the crewmembers complained about my lack of skills. Many of those workers remain my friends today, and we still meet for a beer. Some have asked if I want to come back to work for them. I told them I'd think it over.

21

Not Dead Yet, Just Getting a Third Wind

In 1995, at the age of 57, I was diagnosed with an enlarged prostate. After 11 biopsies over a five-year period, cancer appeared, and I joined a club of men about my age and older who learned that they had the Big C. The treatment options included doing nothing and waiting, implanting radiological pellets, or removing the entire prostate. The medical data at the time were not as clear as I would have liked. Some men live into their nineties with slowly developing prostate cancer and do just fine. Some radiological implants don't work and cause bleeding and pain. The surgery is radical and has several possible long-term consequences, which can include losing sexual function and losing control of bowels and urine. There is also the risk of infection associated with any major surgery.

I talked at length with Cornie and consulted my friends. This was not a simple decision. Even though I was not in any immediate danger, I was a time bomb. And the knowledge of the disease growing inside me became a weight and a distraction. I decided to take the disease out of my body and out of my life by having a radical prostatectomy in 2000 at age 62. After a few months of recovery, I was fabulously lucky and suffered only a few of the adverse consequences that even some of my friends experienced.

My brother Don was not as lucky. In 2010, Don died at the young age of 74. It was way too early for his life to end, and he went through several years of obvious decline and profoundly reduced capacity as a result of Parkinson's disease.

It had taken me a long time to get over the death of my father. At 93, he had lived a wonderfully full and dynamic life. But Don was

179

only 74. He had always, from the earliest days, been there for me. But even with all my money and contacts, I was useless to help him. There was no stopping the reaper.

Don had been tremendously successful in so many aspects of his life. After graduating from Notre Dame, he attended Albany Law School and moved back to Rochester to become a partner in my father's law firm. He later struck out on his own and became a family court judge and the presiding judge for the New York Court of Claims. He was one of the most respected members of New York's legal community. But to me, he was my big brother.

When I was a boy, Don was my rock. As much as I sometimes resented the fact that he always looked after me, I was so glad that he was there to catch me, to guide me, to remind me what I needed to do. Without him, I would have had no daily parental figure in my life. Even when I was a young adult, he was a strong force. He forged a path for me at Notre Dame and helped me to launch my political career at the university—a career that took me to the Kennedy White House. I would never have become the man I am without Don's assistance and his obvious love.

Parkinson's is an ugly disease that can do more than suck the life out of a man; it can also take a man's dignity. But it never took Don's. Even on his deathbed he remained strong, in control, and an icon of integrity and love. I was with him for the week leading up to his passing. He knew the disease was taking him so he planned meticulously to have all of his affairs in order; he didn't want to leave his family in a lurch. He even planned his own funeral. He told me where he wanted the service to be, where he wanted to be buried and how he wanted his life celebrated following his burial and asked me to do the legwork, which I was honored to do.

A few days before he passed, we were out on his front lawn and I could tell that he thought this was perhaps the last time he was going to enjoy such a pleasant day. He looked at the nearby lake and marveled at its beauty. He picked some weeds so that he could look on a perfect garden one last time. And he breathed the fresh air deeply and commented on how sweet it smelled and tasted.

He was not dying. He was living his last days.

Even in death, my brother taught me a valuable lesson: never stop living. As long as you have a breath left in your body, do all you can to enjoy life. And if you're lucky, as my brother was, be a positive force in the lives of your family and the people around you.

After the mall opened in 2001, I kept living life to the fullest, though not as highly accelerated as before. My personal financial behavior changed from taking high risks to growing and protecting assets. It was something of a shift from offense to defense, from being driven by a quest for self-reliance to looking more to others to take the lead. I was out of debt and had a previously unrealized liquid resource that was not going away. So I enjoyed watching others take risks. I watched as friends acquired and developed around the mall site—a site for which value was created by 20 years of walking a tightrope, experiencing loss, and basking in the ultimate success of the new mall.

Outback Corporation acquired the land directly across the street and built a series of restaurants. My neighbor, Joe Taggart, with Crescent Resources, built office buildings on adjacent land and later, my Atlanta friend, Chip Davidson, raised institutional funds and bought all of those buildings from him.

My defensive cash position permitted me to invest smaller amounts in others' projects, while they took the major risks of development in joint-venture deals. I was successful in selecting nicely leveraged opportunities in which my relatively small investment would be worth many times its initial value upon project success. Indeed, I learned to be an investor in projects, rather than a developer, while watching others provide for health care, banking, and back-office ventures.

I had become a different person physically, as well. In the first decade of the twenty-first century, I experienced new physical health issues. They began with the cancer scare and prostate surgery at Hopkins in 2001, which was followed by the insertion of a heart stent in 2003 for a 95% blockage in my left descending artery.

Although my financial health was rock solid, these events created unexpected tensions and conflicts for my body and they managed to settle in my lower back. For 50 years, back pain had been a constant, and I had nearly managed to ignore it. But it was peaking, and I had to turn to aggressive routine of daily yoga therapy, Pilates, stretching, and swimming to help manage the distress.

In 2018 I finally underwent a minimally invasive surgery that eliminated the pain. But in the years leading up to that procedure, I never let the pain get me down, emotionally or physically.

My snow ski trips continued in Aspen and were supplemented by several helicopter ski trips to Western Canada, which required extreme tests of physical ability and risk. I continued to engage in weeks of horseback riding, hunting, and shooting at our beloved Pinckney Hill Plantation and in other locations around the world. In the fall of 2010, I joined Outback Steakhouse's president Paul Avery for a black bear hunt in Montana. The trip reminded me of some of my early life adventures where things had not gone quite as planned. On the bear hunt, we were surprised by a rare encounter with a mountain lion, and later, three timber wolves attacked us. Our young guide had decided to take me to a higher altitude in the Northern Montana woods because I asked for something extra special. I got it. The wolf attack came as we stumbled on a pack killing an elk, and they were not pleased to be interrupted by potential poachers. The guide had only three shells and missed on his first shot, but luckily he hit the two charging wolves, who landed 15 feet below us. We were fortunate to be able to get back to camp that night.

My love of outdoor life was wonderfully enhanced, indeed rewarded with the appointment to the Florida Fish and Wildlife Conservation Commission in 2003. In addition to the thrill of being on the inside of game and wildlife policy in the State of Florida, the commission tenure helped me realize how fabulously fortunate I had been to experience the outdoors intimately in so many different settings. It became vividly clear to me that my own time in the wilderness, throughout my life, had been rare and wonderful. It afforded me opportunities to learn about myself and others within the context of the natural world.

The passion for the importance of youth experiencing the outdoors was reawakened when I saw how much my three oldest children were enjoying Nature's Classroom in Tampa, a day camp where school kids can earn class credit while they are directly exposed to animals in their natural habitats. They get to experience archery, fishing, target shooting, and bird watching, among other nature-based activities. That led to the idea of building a series of youth centers around the state that allow young children the opportunity to experience something beyond their urban neighborhoods, cell phones, and computers. The Florida Youth Conservation Centers allow children from all over Florida—from urban and rural communities, rich and poor—to participate in and learn about the outdoors. As of 2019, there were more than eight centers throughout the state, connecting numerous other nearby outdoor services and facilities.

When I was elected Chairman of the Commission in 2013, it provided me an additional bully pulpit to advocate for the Youth Centers and the associated programs and services.

In helping these children get to know the environment, I have been able to reconnect vividly with the critically important days of my own youth when my father would regularly take me hunting, fishing and canoeing, as I learned about the wilderness and outdoors.

After I retired from the Fish and Wildlife Conservation Commission in 2015, I became a founding board member of the Fish and Wildlife Foundation of Florida, which leads the effort to connect children with traditional outdoor activities, such as fishing, hunting, and camping. Key to the endeavor is developing private-sector interests and identifying land sites around the state of Florida for the youth centers. The first center was made possible by a land gift by our Pinckney Hill Plantation neighbor, Ted Turner. Nearly 20 statewide centers will ultimately be built—and cosponsored by national corporate organizations and individuals. Jim Fowler, my old friend and host of *Wild Kingdom,* was honorary chairperson of this effort. Other states heard about what we were doing and are looking to replicate the model.

If that could be my legacy, it would make me very happy.

CHAPTER 22

Life Comes Full Circle

Around 2010, after my health issues stabilized, I began to feel an uncomfortable *dis-ease*. Something was not right. Indeed, lots of things were not right. My dis-ease was grounded in a personal discomfort with the social, financial, and political events and issues that had taken over the news and the energies of the nation. I became concerned that the world that my father, grandfather, and great-grandfather had struggled to build was being threatened from both the outside and within.

My great-grandfather and grandfather arrived in New York and hit the ground running in order to survive and build a future. There were few, if any, government aid programs, and besides, they had too much self-respect and too much pride in their new homeland to want or even expect a handout. And life was tough. They came to the United States with a belief that it was a place that offered freedoms and opportunities superior to anything else in the world. They believed that the success of an individual and the success of the nation went hand-in-hand, and that if they worked hard and responsibly, they, their families, and their communities would benefit—all of which would serve as a natural, necessary, and powerful foundation for a successful country. And they were correct.

They did not arrive in the United States and demand some dream job, nor did they decide to not work and live off their families—or the government. Instead, they sought to fill a need in the community where they lived. In their case, their community needed barrel makers. They filled that need, provided a valuable service and were afforded fair compensation to support their families, never asking for more than they could earn on their own. Men and women, new immigrants, and people who had lived here for generations, did the same and helped to turn the United States from a nation with the potential for greatness into the greatest nation in the world.

My father's generation—the children of these hard-working immigrants—did not demand a college tuition; they earned it. When my father could not afford to put himself through Notre Dame, he did not look to the federal government for assistance. He looked only to himself, working for several years to make enough money for tuition, and then earning the privilege of attending that university and playing football. This heritage was later documented in Tom Brokaw's book *The Greatest Generation*.

For the most part, my generation took its cues from his, though some *did* appear to lose sight of the role of the individual. How well I remember the 1960s clarion voice of JFK admonishing Americans everywhere: "Ask not what your country can do for you, but what you can do for your country." Jack Kennedy did not invent this philosophy. Generations before him had believed in it. But Kennedy's passion and energy brought the words back to life. A nation is only as strong as its people are willing to make it, and it's also only as strong as its weakest links. I responded to JFK's call and joined his army from the inside.

As I look around today, I listen to the demands and expectations of parts of society and the promises being provided by government that seem to offer, if not ensure, economic equality and security. But in my view, these policies and programs are accomplishing just the opposite for most Americans. Since the 1960s, federal and state governments embarked on an expanding policy of literally giving things away (or promising to) rather than encouraging and enabling people to take responsibility for their lives. My uneducated, economically poor great-grandparents came here with a different model in their heads and hearts, as did millions of East European, Asian, and South American families often giving up land, businesses, and even professions in the old country. Because they didn't speak sufficient English or have the correct license or education, they often became janitors, maintenance staff, carpenters, plumbers, electricians—whatever was needed—wherever they could get work. And they worked relentlessly—often two or more jobs—so that their children could go to school and live better lives. That's what my great-grandparents and grandparents did. It did not, and it cannot, happen overnight. It was not, and is not, because the government awards housing, health care, food stamps, and cell phones. This is not about discrimination, either. My rough-hewn Irish ancestors were often discriminated against because of their religion or national origin.

I firmly believe that a national policy that progressively emphasizes entitlement over earning; that palliates with poorly designed and managed welfare programs without demanding that recipients demonstrate progress toward becoming reliant, kills initiative and the sense of self-worth that drives people to become self-sufficient. This thinking became more than just a reason to rant; it served as a realization that all my life—all the struggles and challenges, the wins and the losses—all those things were just preparation for the things that I could and should dedicate myself to. My brother was right in the early days of the boxing ring when he told me, *Don't quit. Don't give up, if you get knocked down, get back up again.*

I believe the drive for personal success has been draining out of American citizens' hearts, contributing to the financial and political crises that rock our nation. And it led me to ask, *What went wrong?*

Perhaps, I thought, the problem was we hadn't had a leader since JFK to inspire and remind us that hard work, not handouts, built this nation. Perhaps, I felt, it was time that we found a leader who could do that again. I remembered not just the excitement of the Kennedy Camelot days—but also the deeply grounded awareness that I was making a difference in the history of the nation. Fifty years after those pivotal experiences as a young man, I had a renewed and redefined sensibility about what it really takes to build and manage a family, a household, a business and a nation.

All of government, my government, had become clouded. It created more debt than jobs. Goodness, between 2000 and 2008 alone, government and government spending grew wildly and government regulation of the private sector increased. This was done by Democrats *and* Republicans. Then between 2008 and 2013, under President Obama, the nation's debt doubled as the government underwrote new extensive and expensive entitlements.

I decided it was time for me to re-engage in the political process. By not doing so, I would have been denying the commitments and individual contributions that my grandparents had made—and that I had tried to make as a young man. By not re-engaging, it would have been like saying that "I've gotten mine, and I don't care what happens to future generations of my family." I was determined to help get new leadership into the White House—leadership that could turn the ship of this nation around and help guide the nation toward a strong, safe land and renewed strength.

Cornie was not keen on my getting back into politics—and for good reason. For all the years we'd been together, I'd barely had enough time for the family because of business obligations; if I added politics to my schedule, she might as well have been single. But as the government plummeted further and further down what appeared to me to be a socialist hole, I could not sit on the political sidelines any longer. I dusted off my proverbial gloves and jumped back into the ring.

There were half a dozen different candidates to support in 2010, and I was having a hard time deciding which one to get behind. My friend John Rood, with whom I'd served on the Wildlife Commission, told me I needed to meet Mitt Romney. Rood knows politics. In addition to the commission, he has served on the US Department of Housing and Urban Development's Advisory Council on Renewal Communities. In 2009, then-Governor Charlie Crist appointed Rood finance chairman of the Republican Party of Florida and then to the Florida Board of Regents. Rood was well schooled on all of the candidates, their platforms, and their abilities to run a national campaign and then the nation. When he told me that he believed Romney was the right man to lead the country back to its hard-working roots, I decided to check it out for myself.

I met Romney in August 2010. I was in Saratoga Springs, New York and traveled to his home in New Hampshire. I was very impressed with him. He shared the same views as I did on where this nation was going and where it needed to go. I felt especially comfortable with the way he communicated his ideas and philosophy. He was a fellow Harvard MBA and a Baker Scholar, meaning he graduated in the top 5%. And he did so while earning a Harvard law degree. I know how tough a Harvard MBA is to earn. To do so as a Baker Scholar is amazing. To attend law school at the same time is unbelievable! Romney was evidently not a man afraid of hard work. It took very little time after our initial meeting for me to join his campaign as a fundraiser, something I was now uniquely situated and experienced to do.

In November, Mitt and Ann Romney visited Cornie and me at Pinckney Hill and we held a reception that raised his campaign a few hundred thousand dollars. Just as important, Ann and Cornie hit it off as they drove around Pinckney Hill.

I was able to dedicate much of my time to fundraising for Romney. I called friends and colleagues, explained why he was the best man for the job and asked them to donate as much as was allowed, and to call their friends and colleagues and to host fundraisers of their own. In May 2012, I hosted another fundraiser, this time at our home in Avila, raising a quarter of a million dollars. When all was said and done, I raised $3 million for the Romney campaign, money I thought would help lead us, the entire nation, to victory.

I'll never forget the night of the Republican National Convention in Tampa. I sat in one of the suites up high. It was a stark contrast to my first convention as a kid, when I was on the floor as a runner. One thing had not changed: as was the case when I was a 22-year-old college graduate with my life ahead of me, I was swept up by the moment. As I heard Romney speak and I absorbed the crowd's reaction, I got goosebumps and I thought, "This nation can be saved. These people get it." And I was proud of myself for being a part of the process again; I was making a difference and it felt good. Although I wasn't asked, I planned on volunteering to be a part of the transition team. I once again had a dream of being part of the White House to help build a better nation. Obviously, it would be on a different level than I had participated as a young man. I would not be culling applications or even be part of the decision-making process. But I wanted to support the president in any way I could, whether financially or by recommending qualified individuals to fill positions for committees and departments. Just as JFK once inspired people with a desire to get involved, Romney had inspired me.

Then election night came.

I watched the returns with the senior campaign fundraising team in Boston, joined by New York Jets owner Woody Johnson, the Missouri finance chairman, Ambassador Sam Fox, and others. As the results came in, it looked bad. One drink became two, two became three as I tried to drown my sorrows in a glass. A twinge of hope was always in the back of my mind, however. I refused to give up. I refused to believe that more than half of this nation preferred handouts. At around 9 or 10 p.m., however, Donald Trump walked in. I've known Trump since he was a young kid running around New York trying to make his mark. He usually comes across entirely about himself and ego. But when he walked in, he didn't look like his normal, arrogant self. He looked crushed. He looked defeated.

"It doesn't look good," he said.

Sam Fox, a former US Ambassador, looked up at the television as results continued to pour in and agreed with Trump's assessment. When Romney conceded, I sat in stunned silence. Is this what this country had come to? People no longer wanted to earn their way? They wanted a government that supported them without asking for anything in return? Did people really think there was such a thing as a free lunch? Did they not realize that everything they took would have to be paid back by their kids and grandkids for generations? Were they so selfish that they didn't care about the future?

In the weeks following the election, depression sunk in. I mourned for this nation. I took the loss personally, as though I had let my ancestors down, as though I had let my kids and grandkids and future generations down. Then, a friend of mine called and said he had recently been with Mitt Romney. He told me that as they discussed the election and what it meant for the future of the nation, Romney looked him in the eye and said, "I still believe this country can get better."

I was blown away that Romney could still be such an optimist after all he had endured, and I felt pathetic for not being as strong as he was. If he could see a better tomorrow for this nation even after his defeat, I should have as well. He was right. This nation could be saved. I preferred to help do it from the White House, my boyhood dream. But just because I was once again shut out of Capitol Hill didn't mean I should give up on bettering the country.

I decided I would continue to dedicate time, energy, and money to helping to build the type of nation I wanted my kids and grand-kids to live in. If I couldn't do it from the White House, I would do it on my own with my own money. Luckily, soon after the election, I acquired the type of money that would facilitate that commitment.

Never Take Your Eye Off the Ball

In 2012, my eyes were on everything but the International Plaza, a mistake that almost cost me tens of millions of dollars. The plaza had been a stunning success, allowing me to dedicate increasing amounts of time to my family. We took trips around the world. I spent time with my grandson. For the first time, when I told my family that I really wanted them to come first, there was no new, major financial deal or investment waiting to alter the priority list. And I was becoming a different man. My dad's death, my brother's death, my health issues, and being a grandfather had all changed me.

But for a short time, as I got involved in the politics of Romney, everything about the plaza fell completely off my radar screen. I had stopped looking at it as an investment and instead saw it as a possession. The difference between the two is that an investment is there for the sake of making money; it's always for sale if the right opportunity comes along. A possession, by contrast, is yours and only yours, and nothing can rip it from your hands. An investor is always looking for a way to have his asset provide a major return on investment through a sale. But most people don't want to part with their personal property. It gets kind of comfortable. When a developer forgets that one of his developments is an investment and stops paying attention to the marketplace, he stands to lose a lot of money.

Luckily for me, my friends were paying attention to the market and continued to look out for my best interests. This is a rarity in the shark-infested waters of real estate and development: having true friends.

In May 2012, my good friend Chip Davidson, the real estate whiz who purchased three of the buildings surrounding the plaza, called me to kindly tell me to take my head out of the sand. He explained that interest rates were at a near all-time low, which meant individuals and institutions were interested in purchasing safe opportunities and assets. He reminded me that the plaza's worth was at an all-time high and because it was a rare, upscale mall in a unique location—near an airport—economists believed it would remain financially sound, making it a very safe investment. Low interest rates plus a safe investment at its peak value equals the best time to sell. Indeed, Davidson said he was selling many of his assets because they, too, were peaking and advised me to find a buyer for my ownership interest in the plaza before the economy shifted in the other direction.

The International Plaza was my financial baby. I had conceived it, birthed it, and raised it. But it was an investment, not a living being or a possession, which meant no matter how attached I was to it, it was my job to sell it if the right price came along. Davidson insisted I might never find a better price and more suitors than at that moment.

He set me up with an institutional pension fund group in New York City that was so interested that it matter-of-factly said it would pay the maximum price at which the plaza could be valued. They clearly wanted it, but I, of course, always want to negotiate. Sure, I was shaking in delight over this turn of events, but I could not play the role of the interested seller. I knew never to trust anyone when it comes to business negotiations. If I let them know how interested I was, they might have smelled blood, reneged on their original offer to purchase at its highest value, and talked me down. So I told them I would think it over, pretending to be having second thoughts over selling my development baby.

That was the right move to make. But I made the wrong move when I again took my eye off the ball. Shortly after the meeting in New York, Cornie and I were off to Alaska for all of June, and then Aspen in July, and Saratoga in August, which is when I met with Romney. I returned to Tampa for the Republican National Convention and spent some of September in Denmark. I was enjoying life.

When I finally returned to Tampa, I found myself totally immersed in the presidential election. The plaza was the last thing on my mind. In the middle of October, I received a call from Mason Hawkins, a hunting buddy of mine who owns a nearby plantation. He also manages a billion-dollar hedge fund and knows the market as well as anyone. He provided me with the same advice as Davidson:

sell the plaza, because I would never get a better deal for it than I would at that time.

My eye had been way off the ball. Suddenly, the ball struck me right in the face. I realized I had been ignoring a business priority and needed to act before I squandered hundreds of millions of dollars. I called Davidson and without a tinge of "I told you so demeanor," he said, "Dick, Mason is dead right. You need to sell."

Suddenly, I was hit in the face by a second ball—the reality of my business situation. True, I had to sell, but that would be tough to do so while earning an optimized profit. First, if President Barack Obama were reelected (which he was), the capital gains tax would be increased. Certain types of income are taxed at a flat preferential rate, namely long-term capital gains (for example, the gain resulting from the sale of IBM stock or a piece of real estate). Under President George W. Bush, this preferential rate dropped to a near all-time low of 15%.

But effective January 1, 2013, the Bush tax cuts were set to expire. This meant that on that date, the 15% rate automatically reverted to the Clinton-era rate of 20%. In addition, Obamacare also kicked in on January 1 and tacked an extra 3.8% tax on to certain capital gains. The net result would be an increase of 50% in taxes in less than 90 days. If I waited until after the New Year to sell, based on projected values of the plaza, these tax increases would have cost me tens of millions of dollars.

Secondly, and further compounding the matter, I had a contract with my plaza partner, Taubman, stating he had a 90-day right of first offer if I chose to sell my share. It was the middle of October. I could not legally sign a deal with anyone other than Taubman until the middle of January, right after the tax increase.

I was between a rock and a hard place. I wanted to sell, but it appeared Taubman was my only option. This would give Taubman all the negotiating power. And even if I could come to a financial agreement with Taubman, we had to get the deal done quickly. Such deals rarely happen fast.

Davidson calmed me down, saying he would bring in the big guns on this one—Eastdil Secured, which in my mind is the top investment property sales team in the nation. The next thing I know, Eastdil flew four guys into Tampa to meet with me, one from its Washington, DC, office, two from its Atlanta office, and its gem from California, Chris Hoffmann. Hoffmann is the senior managing director of Eastdil Secured LLC and a man who can be a rock if need be in negotiations, yet also knows when to bend. People fear negotiating with him, yet they know he's fair; he makes demands and gets proper value on a deal.

I explained the situation and Hoffmann told me not to worry. He said the founder of Eastdil, Ben Lambert, and Albert Taubman, the patriarch of the mall-development company, had been friends since the 1950s and that Eastdil had represented Taubman in past deals, so there would be a trust in the negotiation room that would help push this deal through more quickly than normal. He said he also knew Taubman's financial portfolio due to past business and would know when they were bluffing and when they were being honest about what they could and could not afford. In addition, he had signed a contract in June with Taubman to buy its partner's 50% interest in the Naples, Florida, mall.

With Eastdil's team in the room, I called Bobby Taubman and told him that I was considering selling my stake in the plaza. Without missing a beat and with excitement in his voice, he said, "Great, we'll give you a good price for it." However, he immediately tempered my excitement by following up with, "We're the only ones who can get that deal done between now and the end of the year, before the capital gains tax goes up." His message: we want to make the deal, but it will be done on our terms because if it's not, you'll lose a lot of money. In other words, "We have you by the balls."

Bobby told me to get on a plane as soon as possible and visit him in Detroit to get the deal done. When I replied that I had to consult with Eastdil first, he paused. He asked me not to bring in a negotiator, insisting we could work the deal out ourselves. I told him I had to do what was best for me and would be in touch soon about setting up a meeting.

Five minutes later I got a call from Steve Eder, Taubman's treasurer and senior vice president, who was in his car on his way to La Guardia Airport. He had tipped the company's hand. They wanted this deal done even more than I did. Otherwise, he could have waited to call me. He said he was going to look over the finances as soon as he was back in Detroit and that he was positive we could come to an agreement. When I told him that any agreement would have to be okayed by Eastdil, he was silent for a few moments before responding in a tone of hushed shock, "Oh, my god." He said he would call me back. Ten minutes later, he did, and before I could even say hello, he asked, "Dick, what have you done with Eastdil?" When I explained that I had engaged Chris Hoffmann to represent me on the deal, he was again silent. Then, he said, "Dick, you've just gotten the one person in the country we respect. He's also the best. Congratulations. Now come visit us."

Just like that, the ball was back in my court.

Several days before the presidential election in November, Hoffmann and I flew to Detroit for the meeting. We sat in one of Bobby Taubman's conference rooms and, though we were old friends at that point, and didn't bother with any small talk. We got right down to business. "Dick, what is it that you want?" Bobby asked.

Without flinching, I declared, "One billion dollars."

This, I must explain, was not what I wanted my profit to be. We needed to set a price for what the plaza was worth. And I believed it to be worth a billion dollars. Taubman and I were 50-50 partners on the development. Once the plaza's worth was settled, Taubman would pay me half of that. I wanted to walk away with half a billion dollars.

Taubman, also not flinching, responded, "You're absolutely crazy."

To which Hoffmann shot back, "Well, Dick shoots high. What do you offer?"

This is what makes Hoffmann so effective. He made it seem like he was on their side. We both knew they weren't going to jump at my first offer and would respond with what we considered a low-ball counter, but by seeming like he agreed with them, it would make it easier to counter their offer with a higher and more fair one. They're expert businessmen themselves, so I'm sure Taubman and his executives knew the game, but while in negotiations we all played along and pretended to be ignorant about what was really going on. Perhaps it would be quicker to cut right to the finality, but where is the fun in that? Remember, big business is not always about the dollars and cents; it's also about the high and the rush of making the deal and fighting for every penny. It's not *like* a sporting event— it *is* a sport. We pine for that final score, but the game itself is what we enjoy.

Taubman countered with $825 million. I thought that was unacceptable. They explained their numbers, we split hairs over some of the nuances, and then called it a day, no closer to a deal than we had been at the start of the meeting.

As Hoffmann and I walked out of the room, Taubman hurried after us, inviting me over for dinner. He walked us all the way to our car, waiting for me to say yes. I told him I was on my way to visit one of his neighbors who was involved in the Romney inaugural planning, so perhaps I would stop by after. While Hoffmann drove to the airport, I was driven separately to the neighbor's office.

But I had barely walked through his door when my cell phone rang. It was Hoffmann. "Get the hell out of there right now," he stated firmly when he found out where I was. "Walk out of that door and catch a flight home immediately." And that's what I did. Much to Taubman's surprise, I hung up the phone and told him I needed to be back in Tampa immediately, said my goodbyes, and caught the next flight home.

Again, it's all a game, no different from men and women courting one another. They want to play it cool, act like they're not as interested as they actually are, knowing that doing so will pique the other's interest even more. We always want what we think we can't have. I may have a mind for analyzing the potential of a development, but I'm not skilled at hiding my true intentions. Hoffmann was right in telling me to get out of there. I needed to leave before I showed my poker hand. It got Taubman thinking, "Why did he have to fly back to Tampa so quickly? Does he have another suitor?" He knew that if I found someone willing to say yes to the billion-dollar deal, even with the loss from the capital gains tax, I would have walked away with more money than I would with his offer.

Taubman immediately called his friend, Eastdil's CEO Roy March, with whom he normally dealt. He hoped that by appealing to a friend he could get some movement on the deal. No luck. March was not going to compromise a top partner's negotiation. He trusted Hoffmann's instincts. March told Taubman that it was up to Hoffmann and me and that unless we could find a middle ground he doubted a deal would be made.

Meanwhile, Romney lost the election and I fell into a pit of depression. Not only did I think our nation would never find its way, but I knew that the capital gains tax was definitely going up. I was screwed. I either had to make a deal with Taubman or lose tens of millions of dollars in profits.

Hoffmann again told me not to panic. He said that as long as we continued to engage other suitors, one of two things would happen: we could find one willing to pay substantially more than Taubman, negating the $30 million loss; or we could scare Taubman into thinking someone was going to agree with our billion-dollar assessment, forcing him to up his offer.

Hoffmann found a pension fund that agreed to $950 million. However, before I could pump my fist for the victory, the potential buyer hit me with a major *but*, claiming the restrictions on my agreement with Taubman were too stringent and needed to be loosened if it was going to become partners with Taubman. I won't bore you with the details of what needed to be changed; nor do I think I need to explain why Taubman wouldn't agree to the changes. What matters is that if the changes weren't made, the pension fund said it would pay only $875 million. But even with the capital gains tax loss, the deal would earn me an estimated $50 million more than Taubman's offer. We were making some progress.

Hoffmann told me to hold off on making a deal. He thought we could do better. He had been tipped off that Taubman had contacted Metropolitan Life, which held the mortgage on the plaza, and told them to begin the process of changing the mortgage. For the sale to be made, Met Life had to give its approval. There was no doubt that it would, but it takes time for all the paperwork to be filed. That meant that Taubman was going to give in and up his offer and wanted to get the paperwork filed immediately, knowing if he waited and the deal wasn't completed until after the new year, he would have to offer even more money to make up for the $50 million I would lose.

Minutes after Hoffmann explained this to me, literally minutes, Bobby Taubman called him asking if I had come to my senses. I don't know if he had inside knowledge of the other offer or if it was just a coincidence. Hoffmann did not budge, explaining we had other interested buyers offering more. Taubman also had no idea that Hoffmann was aware of the Met Life dealings, which put Hoffmann in full control of these negotiations.

A few days later, Taubman called Hoffmann again, this time offering $875 million. It equaled the other offer, but we could get this one done before the capital gains tax went up, which meant I would walk away with an optimized profit. But I still had one problem with the offer. I was worried that Taubman was going to purchase my half of the mortgage and then turn around and sell it for a greater profit. I'd had an offer of $950 million if restrictions were loosened. I feared he could loosen the restrictions and find a buyer for $950 million or more.

I know many would laugh at an already wealthy man not being satisfied with $875 million. But business is not always about money. It's about the high of the deal and it's about *ego*. Businessmen always want to walk away from a deal believing that they got the better of it. If Taubman sold my half for more, I would be seen as the loser in the deal. My ego could not allow that to happen.

Taubman understood this. He knew me and knew how he would feel on the other end of this deal. He offered anywhere from $7.5 to $12.5 million if he sold my half of the mortgage within the next 18 months. I countered that offer: if he sold, I would leave the total amount he paid me up to him. I have an ego, but I also know that to get, you have to give. This was my way of telling Taubman I trusted him and that I hoped the tough negotiations had not damaged our friendship. He told me that my trusting him to pay a reasonable amount was a testimony to both his father's philosophy and the substance of the relationship that had resulted in one of the most successful malls Taubman had ever built. Our deal was done.

The only remaining hurdle was Met Life. Though Taubman had begun the process already, the company has a history of taking its time and I had about $30 million from the capital gains tax on the line. When Taubman told them that the deal was done and all we were waiting for was a review, my friend Chuck Davis, who runs Met Life Real Estate Investments in Atlanta, told Taubman that he would get everything completed before the end of December because he "really likes Dick Corbett."

On December 19, the deal was finalized. I received $437 million.

As I sat down that night and looked back on all the events in my life that had led to that monumental moment, I realized the irony of it. My business career was launched when my dream of helping the nation from the White House was dashed following Bobby Kennedy's assassination. Years later, that same political dream was dashed again but led to an epic event in my business career. If Romney had won the election, I would have been busy helping him in whatever way I could; I would not have taken the time to get involved in working out the final details of the plaza sale.

A friend told me that with the type of money I had, if I wasn't happy with the direction of the nation, I could afford to direct my time and energy to improving it. Years ago, that might very well have been an exclusively ego-driven thought. The United States is my country, and I have never been more aware of the importance of contributing to its value. I'm proud of the successes I've enjoyed and the opportunity to find Cornie and raise a family with her.

I owe some of my accomplishments to the ghost of Joseph Kennedy. Studying his financial records late after work each night when everybody had left the office afforded insight into how he maneuvered and strategized financially and politically. The documents I used to study after business hours at the Kennedy office have probably not been read by many people in the decades since he achieved his success. But the Old Man provided me with inspiration and a vision of what was possible for me. Joe Kennedy's Merchandise Mart in Chicago was a guiding concept for the International Plaza—all the while knowing and understanding that Kennedy got there through hundreds of small deals, failures, and lots of time.

Far more important for me than the Kennedy saga is the very tangible and real story of my family. My ancestors helped to build this country from the ground up, with personal sacrifice, hard work, and a belief that made a difference.

After watching Mitt Romney's response to his election loss, when he said that America is a great nation and will overcome the challenges we face, I was at first embarrassed about my anger, but then inspired to agree with him. My brother Don's message added to this: no stopping, no giving up, make everything count—not just for me, but for my family first, and then, if and when I can, for the greater community.

Epilogue: More of What's Important, Not More of the Same

This epilogue is a reflection of my intent to share my story and lessons learned with my progeny and others.

I learned after high school that the boxing ring was something I took with me wherever I went. It was one of my first real passions, and its ropes and mat were the first pieces of real estate I felt I could own and control.

I've told this story from my unabashedly selfish, subjective point of view, to write what my wife, Cornelia, jokingly calls my ego-ography. I have not dedicated my life to unselfishly giving back, as Cornie has. I have instead been motivated by and consumed with using capitalism to obtain independence, security, and personal fulfillment. That is what used to be called "the American Dream." In pursing and realizing that dream, I believe that I bettered my adopted hometown of Tampa, Florida—a community that afforded me the opportunity to move from welterweight to heavyweight matches.

The boxing ring is where I learned as a boy to fight and engage the world. It was both freeing and limiting. It became a part of me and helped to build tremendous strengths and desires—but it also helped to make me a prisoner, within its ropes, of my own fears, expectations, and wants.

My evolved and practiced emotional mask enabled me to hide my fears from friends, family, and business associates during times when I was not certain I could overcome whatever obstacle was in my way. I became adept at not losing the backing of those I needed to have in my corner if I was to succeed. I could not expect to take down an opponent in the ring if he sensed fear, doubt, or distraction on my face. Should doubt and mistrust surface, it becomes difficult to win back the confidence and trust from others that is needed to secure collaboration and agreements to provide financial and political support.

The natural world is dangerous, and the niceties of packaged civilization don't always apply. Snakes, bears, undercurrents in streams, and bad weather have no compassion and take no prisoners. Sometimes, perhaps most of the time, I believed that people were just as ruthless, by nature—and that deal making was, by nature, a ruthless sport—nothing personal. In the real estate game, as was the case each time I entered the boxing ring, I had to proceed with the deep-seeded assumption that failure was not an option.

I learned very early that it's easy to throw a punch—but taking one and remaining in the fight is what separates the winners from the losers. I learned to wake up every morning anticipating that somebody was going to throw, and possibly land, a left hook at me. I needed to strategize, in advance, what my optional responses would be—just as was the case in the ring. Second and third guessing in business is as essential to avoid a crippling punch.

I also learned from boxing to graciously accept that a winning strategy may come from someone else, and not to be too proud to take advice from others. Some people are too arrogant, foolish, or unable to learn from experience, and are unwilling or unable to accept advice from others.

Amazon will not deliver success to your doorstep. You have to fearlessly (but not blindly) chase it. But be wary of who you trust and what you expect. This can require circumstantial learning for each person. But I can tell you that it's easy to get swept up in a presumed "friendship" with a powerful person. You'll want to believe they have your best interests at heart, in part because believing that such people are "friends" boosts your ego. But don't let their power blind you to their basic nature. Not all other businesspeople could be trusted with my future. But I did learn that there is an inner circle of loyal, caring people who have remained steadfast keys to my success, and sometimes my piece of mind. These include my wife, Cornelia Corbett, Melanie Craig, Jennifer Kent, Chip Davidson, Dick Greco, and Jay Wolfson. And sometimes, those few, inner-circle people will be brutally candid, and it may hurt—but they have won my trust. Remember, it is a two-way street—*be there* for your inner circle of family and friends.

Sometimes I wonder if my successes came at a cost.

I always had a sense of rush, rush, rush; do, do, do; focus, focus, focus—rarely taking the time to appreciate what I'd already accomplished, or who may have affected along the way. I would achieve success after success with real estate deals. But rather than step out of the ring and stand back for a bit to take the time to appreciate what I did, I'd *immediately* think, "Now what? I want to do more! Where is the next deal?" After the huge financial success of my biggest deal, I still had a feeling of emptiness.

For years Cornie has tried to get me to stop to smell the roses. She'd tell me to appreciate what I have done and not linger on what I haven't done. She had more confidence and a better-grounded sense of self and was hoping to attach me to her anchor.

I was raised by a father who worked too hard and too much. I saw firsthand how his overzealous work habits and drive had a negative effect on our family. But the apple does not fall far from the tree. I did many of the same things he did—and I often put my obsession for work over attention to my children. Could I have been there for my children in ways other than providing wealth?

As my children became young adults, I wondered if my success would dampen theirs—would they have the same grit and drive and need and will to work as I did? Could they earn their way into success as I defined it?

As I take this stroll outside of the ring, I realize that I may have judged my children incompletely. I probably expressed my view that if they did not do as I had, they were weak. I was often critical and suggested that they might be lazy. My dreams and my expectations were my metrics for them. I did not think to ask about their dreams or expectations.

It has taken me a while to *want* to listen and to hear what they have to say. I'm still working on that. They are blessed, and I should be proud to have helped to create, with Cornie, a rich, dynamic life for them with infinite opportunities. I caught my white whale early enough in life that I now have time to enjoy the ride. I can't recoup the lost time or the lost opportunities. But I can try to create time and connection now.

I worked hard because I was driven by my past. I worked hard because I was *personally* fearful of financial failure, which I equated with getting knocked out in a fight. I worked hard because I wanted to, and because it provided fulfillment. I saw every deal as a new bout in a new ring and a continuing opportunity to prove to myself and others that I could still fight and win. I have taken the ring with me wherever I went and made all encounters, all deals, all relationships another round in a championship fight that never ends. I needed to have independent financial success and security, and I accomplished that. I needed and wanted to prove to myself that I could fight and win, even after weathering some very tough punches.

I was part of Camelot. And I was on the road to being king of the mountain!

Then the earthquake of Bobby's assassination left me under a landslide, sitting alone in a Los Angeles morgue, wearing a robe, with Bobby lying in a coffin in front of me, in my clothes. I had been stripped naked, literally and emotionally. I had no idea what I was going to do next and I retreated into my sorrows and uncertainties. But then I bounced back and refocused.

Bobby Kennedy is, indeed, buried in my clothes. And my hopes and dreams could have been buried with him. I wanted so much to remain part of the Kennedy mystique, the high political stakes, the rushes of political deal making, the glamor of Camelot.

But there was the other Kennedy world—of business and land deals and strategic investments. I pivoted from Camelot toward the amazingly pragmatic world of the Merchandise Mart and the Kennedy financial engines designed by Old Man Joe. I found my passion in development—in the deals, the bickering, the dollars, and the monuments of successful real estate. It was that passion that enabled me to become one of the best of my era. The personal and political strategizing I had learned in the rings of Rochester, Notre Dame, the White House, and Bobby's campaign all came together in real estate development. Each deal was a bout in a new ring and a campaign requiring political, financial, and social skills, prowess, luck, and help from others.

About the Author

Richard **A. Corbett** is considered a leading real estate investor and developer. Corbett's commitment to economic development and growth management are reflected in the more than $1 billion in complex real estate ventures that he has financed, developed, and constructed. They have all involved the crafting of delicate political and financial relationships with local and national financial institutions, investment partners, and government bodies. In 2001, Corbett built International Plaza—a mixed-use retail, office, and hotel development of approximately 3 million square feet—located at the Tampa International Airport. The mall has over 18 million visitors a year. It has generated thousands of permanent jobs, hundreds of new commercial sales groups, office space, adjunct hotels and restaurants, and produces hundreds of millions of dollars annually for the regional economy. Corbett was a presidential aide in the John F. Kennedy administration and subsequently was employed by the Kennedy family in managing their real estate trust portfolio in New York City. Corbett is married to Cornelia G. Corbett. They have four children and five grandchildren.

Index